THE FACULTY PARKING LOT IS NOT FOR PLANNING

BECOMING AN EFFECTIVE FIRST-YEAR TEACHER

James L. Conro

Rowman & Littlefield Education
Lanham • New York • Toronto • Plymouth, UK

Published in the United States of America
by Rowman & Littlefield Education
A Division of Rowman & Littlefield Publishers, Inc.
A wholly owned subsidary of The Rowman & Littlefield Publishing
Group, Inc.
4501 Forbes Boulevard, Suite 200, Lanham, Maryland 20706
www.rowmaneducation.com

Estover Road
Plymouth PL6 7PY
United Kingdom

British Library Cataloguing in Publication Information Available

Library of Congress Cataloging-in-Publication Data

Conro, James L.
  The faculty parking lot is not for planning : becoming an effective
first-year teacher / James L. Conro.
      p. cm.
  Includes bibliographical references and index.
  ISBN-13: 978-1-57886-504-8 (pbk. : alk. paper)
  ISBN-10: 1-57886-504-2 (pbk. : alk. paper)
  1. First year teachers—In-service training—United States. 2. Teachers—
Training of—United States. 3. Teacher effectiveness—United States.
I. Title.
  LB2844.1.N4C66 2006
  371.1—dc22   2006016508

⊗™ The paper used in this publication meets the minimum requirements
of American National Standard for Information Sciences—Permanence of
Paper for Printed Library Materials, ANSI/NISO Z39.48-1992.
Manufactured in the United States of America.

This book is dedicated to the following Master Teachers, with whom it was such an honor to work:

Cynthia Alkire
Robert Bibby
Cindy Campbell
Lloyd Dudley
Gordon Gifford
Peter Holmen
Drew Jaffe
Evelyn Kwasniewski
Robert Riccio
Norma McNally
Jeannette Morgan
Ruth Pabich
Phillip Paulson
Wayne Schlegel
Claudia Soares
Barbara Starkie

Dale Amundson
Mark Chabot
Onil Couture
Wilfred Duchesneau
Elvin Fleming
T. J. Gallagher
Suzanne Higney
Arnold Howe
Lois Johnson
Scott Moody
Elizabeth Rhyner
Michael Rudd
Robert Slajda
Bruce Stark
Lynn Waldo

This book is also dedicated to the memory of Lloyd Dudley and Phil Paulson, two devoted teachers who loved their students and displayed their love of teaching daily. They will always be remembered by their colleagues and certainly will never be forgotten by their students, whose hearts they touched.

CONTENTS

PREFACE   vii

1   CLASSROOM MANAGEMENT   1

2   FOUR ESSENTIAL COMPONENTS   19

3   TEACHING TO THE OBJECTIVE   41

4   TEACHING FOR RETENTION   57

5   TEACHING FOR TRANSFER   67

6   EVALUATION   77

7   EFFECTIVE TEACHING RESEARCH   93

8   PUTTING IT TOGETHER   101

REFERENCES   109

ABOUT THE AUTHOR   111

PREFACE

Although this book will provide veteran teachers with some useful reminders, it is primarily intended to be a how-to manual for new teachers. Each chapter is devoted to presenting the best practices employed by the most successful classroom teachers and supported by educational research.

The book was written in plain language and highlights real classroom examples from actual classroom situations. The successful techniques are discussed step-by-step from preparation for the first day of school through lesson preparation, assessment, a review of important research on teaching, and putting it all together.

The book begins with a chapter devoted to classroom management, as that is essential for any teaching and learning to occur. The most effective techniques are discussed, and classroom management strategies are presented. The chapter includes a review of the most important points in successful classroom management and concludes with activities to prepare for the first day in the classroom.

Chapter 2 takes the reader through designing a lesson containing the four most essential elements: an initial sponge activity, a statement of the lesson's objective(s), frequent checks to ensure student understanding, and closure at the end of the period.

Chapter 3 looks at teaching to a specific objective: how to teach to your objective(s), the role of effective questioning techniques, and developing effective questions.

Chapters 4 and 5 illustrate how to promote retention and transfer by properly structuring your lessons with mnemonic devices and effective examples. Chapter 6 looks at the connections between the objectives, homework, and evaluation. Chapter 7 examines the volumes of research on effective teaching over the past twenty years. The reader should note the similarity between the actions of the most successful teachers and the recommendations of the research.

In each chapter, the examples are taken from real classrooms in elementary, middle, and high schools. The examples provided are used by the most successful of classroom teachers. The chapters conclude with a review of the essential points for the classroom teacher to remember in building a lesson. Many chapters also feature activities for the new teacher to assist in preparing for the classroom.

The final chapter takes the new teacher step-by-step through the planning of an actual classroom lesson.

1

CLASSROOM MANAGEMENT

Without an appropriate classroom atmosphere, learning cannot occur. Above all, an effective teacher is skilled in classroom management. The primary reason for which teachers are released or dismissed is not because they lack knowledge in either the subject matter or teaching techniques. Generally, nearly every teacher who is not successful in the classroom lacks classroom management skills. Simply put, if you cannot manage your classroom, you cannot teach!

Prior to walking into the classroom for the first time as a new teacher thirty-seven years ago, I was given some advice by an experienced colleague: "Do not smile until Thanksgiving. You can always ease up once you have control. It is not easy to tighten down after you lose control of a class." Although "do not smile until Thanksgiving" is a bit of an overexaggeration, the point about it being easier to ease up than to tighten down is very valid. New teachers who have been too lax in classroom management have found it extremely difficult to regain control.

Successful teachers are in control of their classrooms from the first day of classes. They have an established procedure, which includes:

- Calling the class to order when the bell rings.
- Taking roll, assigning seats, and making a seating chart.
- Posting and explaining the classroom rules.
- Distributing a course syllabus that indicates the textbook(s) and replacement costs, academic and behavioral expectations, the grading system, and major required projects.
- Ending with the assignment for the next class meeting, and an understanding of the assignment and the materials needed for class.

Classroom rules need to be posted and must be visible and clearly readable from every seat in the room. Limit your classroom rules to six or fewer, and include each of the following categories:

- Start of class. (Be in the room when the bell rings.)
- Interaction. (Raise your hand to talk to/answer the teacher.)
- End-of-class. (The teacher, not the bell, dismisses the class.)
- Class-specific. (Rules covering bathroom passes, food, etc.)

Successful teachers are effective classroom managers because they not only post clear classroom rules but also explain and teach the rules and procedures and identify specific consequences. They also are consistent in enforcing all building rules in and out of their classroom.

Classroom rules are highly important and need to be discussed the first day. It is essential that the teacher present a serious attitude in explaining the classroom rules and procedures. If the teacher jokes about the rules, the students will not take them seriously. It is recommended that the teacher:

- Explain each rule. (For example, if a rule is "one student out of the room at a time," explain that only one student may be out of the room at a time, whether at the office, drinking fountain, or lockers, and that the permanent pass is hanging next to the door. If the permanent pass is not hanging next to the door, a student is out of the room with the pass. Any student wanting to use the pass will need to wait until the student—and the pass—return.)
- Give a student-focused rationale for each rule. (For example, "Raise your hand so that only one student talks at a time, allowing everyone to hear what was said.")
- Clearly identify the consequences for breaking the rules. (For example, students may lose the privilege of leaving the room with the permanent pass.)

Teachers who are not successful in classroom management may very well have done all of the above; the reason they are less than successful in managing a classroom and have lost the respect of their students is often that they have failed to follow the two most important rules pertaining to discipline:

- The discipline must be fair and consistent (and followed up).
- The discipline must be done with dignity and respect.

These two points will be further explained later in this chapter.

At the bottom of the posted classroom rules, it does not say, "These rules will not be enforced." Nor does it say, "Enforced on an inconsistent basis." This, however, is sometimes the case and is the major reason that some teachers are unsuccessful classroom managers.

Students need and prefer structure. They must also have consistency. The inconsistent enforcement of classroom rules confuses students. If a rule is only enforced occasionally, the students do not know what is, and is not, permissible.

Examples of inconsistency are:

- Enforcing some rules and ignoring the infractions of other rules.
- Disciplining some students for minor infractions while overlooking major rule violations by others.

The most glaring example of the latter that this author personally witnessed was in an English classroom. The teacher inappropriately sent a student to the office for a minor infraction (dropping a pencil), while totally ignoring a student who swore directly at the teacher. No matter what the posted rules for that classroom stated, this clearly indicated to the students that such language to the teacher is permissible in that class. On a daily basis, the rules must be enforced consistently. The same infractions have to result in the same consequences for each and every student every day of the school year. There are not different rules for different students. The same rules apply to all students. It is also essential that every teacher enforce all building rules in every classroom. Any classroom teacher who ignores a building rule (for example, overlooking a student's lateness to class) is being grossly unfair and inconsiderate of all of the other teachers in the building. You do not want the students telling teachers, "We can do that in Mr. ___'s room." A teacher cannot pick and choose from the building rules. The enforcement of all rules is part of the job.

Master teachers seldom send students out of their class; they manage students that other teachers may consider to be discipline problems. These teachers are successful because:

- Students are all treated with respect and dignity.
- Students are kept on task throughout the class period.
- Student lag time during transitions is minimized.
- Students know the consequences for breaking classroom rules.

- Students know that the rules are enforced on a consistent basis.
- Students who fail to have a book or pencil are provided with one to use for the class period.

The above points will be examined and explained in further detail later in the chapter.

Successful teachers use a variety of subtle techniques to prevent minor discipline problems. They do not demean or humiliate their students. They do not issue ultimatums or challenge a student in front of the student's peers. They do not engage in lengthy debates about what the student did or did not do. They do not raise their voice in class. They do not belittle the student or his or her older siblings whom the teacher also taught. All of these behaviors are characteristic of the less-than-successful classroom teacher. Some highly effective techniques utilized by successful teachers to maintain an appropriate classroom environment are:

- Signals. An off-task student may be silently corrected. A finger pressed vertically to the lips will stop a student from talking to a friend. The teacher making eye contact and simply shaking his or her head may do the same. In either case, the correction can be made without the teacher saying a word to the student and without interrupting the class.
- Proximity. An off-task student may also be corrected silently if the teacher moves into a position next to that student's desk. The nearness of the teacher to the student sends a message that is clearly understood; again, the class is not interrupted.
- Verbal signals. Effective classroom teachers also use short verbal signals to correct students who are off task. By making eye contact with the student and calling him or her by name, and then continuing, the teacher has again sent a clear message. It is quick. It is simple. There is no need for the teacher to elaborate. The amount of class

time lost is minimized. Generally, this action is sufficient; if not, or if the student replies, "What?" move on to the next technique.

- Verbal direction. The purpose of this technique is to calmly indicate to the student that the inappropriate behavior will not be tolerated. Again, the teacher makes eye contact, calls the student by name, and adds, "You need to work on ___." No matter what the response from the student is (unless agreement), the teacher repeats the original direction, "You need to work on ___."
- If the inappropriate behavior continues after the above actions, an effective classroom teacher would take the student aside and invoke a consequence, generally, a teacher detention. Inform the student to "See me after class." This is considerably more effective than saying "This is a detention." By announcing to the entire class that the student has a detention, the teacher has now formally challenged that student in front of his or her peers. The student will have to respond to this challenge, resulting in a disruption in the learning. This can be avoided by talking to the student after class and assigning the detention in private. After the class, inform the student that he or she has a detention and the reason for the detention.

A less-than-successful classroom teacher would take one of the following inappropriate actions:

- Do nothing. The teacher does not assign a detention. The classroom rules become meaningless because there are no consequences for breaking them! Without consequences, the teacher has no credibility and has lost control of the classroom.
- Send the student to the office. Ask yourself, "Is this appropriate? Does this warrant sending the student to the office?"

Effective classroom teachers rarely send students to the office; when they do send a student out of the classroom, it is never for a minor infraction. Effective classroom teachers send students out of the room for major infractions only, not trivial ones such as not having a book or pencil, not having homework completed, not being on time for class, or not being on task.

Effective teachers do not push all of their classroom discipline off on the building's assistant principal. They do not clog up the assistant principal's office with their students due to minor infractions that can be dealt with in the classroom. Effective teachers also file a "disciplinary referral" every time a student is sent to the office; sending the student out of class is a reward for his or her behavior—it is not a consequence. If the student's behavior was so inappropriate that it warranted being sent out of the room, then it warrants a consequence. By completing a "disciplinary referral" for the assistant principal or principal, a process is initiated that will result in disciplinary action. The teacher is not doing the student a favor by failing to file a disciplinary referral. When completing the disciplinary referral form, be sure to give the appropriate information in sufficient detail. "Disruptive" is not specific! Provide details of how the student was disruptive. Instead of "inappropriate language," for example, provide the specific, inappropriate language that the student used.

- Overreact. A less-than-successful teacher may also overreact and escalate a minor infraction by demeaning or humiliating the student (even to the extent of using words such as "stupid" or "useless"), yelling, or delivering a lengthy lecture. With any of these reactions, the teacher has broken one of the major rules regarding discipline by not treating the student with respect and dignity. The teacher has also lost the respect of the class.

Some examples of appropriate consequences:

INCIDENT	CONSEQUENCE
Student arrives tardy to class.	Have the student sign in. Assign a detention for each tardy or for a predetermined number of tardies.
Student does not have a pencil and/or textbook.	Maintain a supply of textbooks and pencils in your classroom. Have the students sign for the use of these items for the period.
Student is talking while the teacher or another student is talking.	If the student is responding to a question or commenting on the discussion, ignore the student's comments. Remind the student of the rule. If the problem persists, assign a teacher detention. Call the parents if this continues.
Student leaves at the end of the period prior to being dismissed (or stands at the door).	Have the student return to his or her seat. Dismiss the rest of the class at the bell, but talk to the student long enough for every other student to have left. The student will understand the message.
Student talks during the announcements.	Remind the student of the rule. Change his or her seat. If the problem persists, assign a teacher detention.

Student does not turn in an assignment on time.	Reduce the grade by a predetermined percentage each day. This should be noted in your distributed syllabus. If the situation persists, call the parents.
Inappropriate items in class.	Confiscate the items (toys, cell phones, CD players, iPods, Blackberrys, etc.). Lock them in a secure place. The student may pick the item up on the last day of school. A parent may pick the item up before that date.
Inappropriate attire.	Notify the building administrator. Provide the name of the student and identify the item of clothing.
Inappropriate language to the teacher.	Inform the student to see you after class. Tell the student that his behavior will not be tolerated and assign a teacher detention. Call the parents. If the language is obscene, notify the office immediately and send the student out.
Persistent problems.	Request a conference with the parent and contact the student's counselor.

One of the items reviewed above was "inappropriate attire" worn by the students, which recently has become a concern in schools nationwide. It would be remiss to not discuss the importance of appropriate attire on the part of teachers. Simply put, teachers are professionals; as such, teachers need to dress as professionals. The distinction between student and teacher should be visible in their respective attire! You are *not* a student; do not dress like one. This does not require a suit and tie or a dress daily, but the dress code should be semiformal, not casual. Acceptable attire would include a suit, sport coat (tie optional) or sweater, and dress slacks for males; a dress, skirt and blouse, or suit for females. Unacceptable attire includes T-shirts, shorts, and jeans (unless your school has a "dress-down" day).

Another outstanding characteristic of effective teachers in handling student discipline is the fact that they communicate with parents. Consider a scenario in which a meeting is held in December to discuss a student's behavior in class. At the meeting, the teacher complains that the inappropriate behavior has been occurring "for months." Logically, the parents will ask, "Why is this the first we are hearing about it? Why did you not call when the problem began?" How would you respond to the parents?

Effective classroom teachers never have to respond to such a question, as it is never asked of them. If it is necessary to give a student a second teacher detention, it is time to contact the parents. As a teacher, never hesitate to contact a parent. If you receive a response that is less than positive, request a meeting and ask your supervisor to attend that meeting. In this electronic age with computers and e-mail, there is no longer any excuse for not being able to reach parents, such as not being able to reach them by phone or the absence of an answering machine. Successful teachers share their e-mail address with parents through their course syllabus or at an annual open house for parents. They encourage the parents of their students to share e-mail addresses with the teacher.

Contacting a parent or guardian can be scary for new teachers; you will, however, find that the vast majority of the parents are totally supportive of the teachers and the school. Do *not* hesitate to initiate contact with parents. It is one of the best moves a new teacher can make. It is advisable to begin the conversation by introducing yourself and making some positive comments about the student, and then explain the current problem, indicating that you wish to work with the parent in order that the student be successful.

It is inevitable that sooner or later you will run into the rare irate parent. The best advice is to schedule a meeting with the parent and have a department chair or administrator attend the meeting. Do not "brave it" alone!

A common cause of disruptions and inappropriate off-task student behavior is "lag time." Lag time is any time students are not actively engaged. In many classes, the beginning and end of the period are lag time; as such, this time is completely unproductive. Effective classroom teachers eliminate any lag time at the beginning and end of the period with a "sponge activity" at the start of the class and an effective student-focused closure at the end. Both of these activities will be discussed in detail later.

Effective teachers also minimize the amount of lag time during transitions as they proceed from one activity to another by:

- Posting an agenda for the period on the chalkboard. This shows the students what the activities for the period are. They know throughout the class period what the next activity will be.
- Announcing the transition. The teacher will state that it is time to move to the next activity. Many effective teachers will also count down to this change, by periodically indicating

the number of minutes or seconds until the change of activities occurs.

- Giving clear and specific directions. Directions that include more than three steps should be written and remain visible throughout the activity. Specific directions include, "Put this away now. When everyone is ready, all of the teams will turn to page 120 and graph problem number twelve." If there are more than two problems, write the numbers on the chalkboard. It will prevent the problem numbers from having to be repeated several times.

The key to minimizing lag time during transitions is organization. Lag time frequently results in inappropriate behavior, as the students are not on task. The effective teacher reduces the amount of off-task time, thereby reducing the opportunity for inappropriate behavior.

Although it may seem strange to include chalkboard use in a discussion on classroom management, it definitely has a direct bearing on this area. Even in an age where overhead projectors, computers, and in-focus projectors are used regularly, the chalkboard or whiteboard is still used daily in most classrooms. In many rooms it is used in an ineffective manner.

When a teacher writes on the chalkboard, his or her back is to the class. With the teacher's back to the class, and eyes on what is being written, the teacher obviously cannot view the class. With the teacher's back to the class, the teacher is virtually giving the students an invitation to do whatever they want. It is an invitation to inappropriate behavior. The object is to minimize the amount of time that the teacher's back is turned while writing on the chalkboard.

Less-than-successful teachers virtually "talk to the chalkboard" and are oblivious as to what is happening behind them in the classroom. This is not only poor classroom management but poor teaching as well. The teacher, obviously, needs to talk to the students, not to the chalkboard. Eye contact should be made between the teacher and the students while talking, not between the teacher and the chalkboard. Proper use of the chalkboard provides for appropriate classroom management and also provides for the needs of both auditory and visual learners.

The rules are very simple:

- *Say it.* Face the students, not the chalkboard. Say the word(s) or phrase(s) that you are going to write on the chalkboard.
- *Write it.* Turn around and write the same word(s) or phrase(s) on the chalkboard that you spoke. The students are processing what you said and writing it down while you are writing the words on the chalkboard. Therefore, while your back is turned they are occupied by writing, and the act of writing reinforces the learning.

The above process allows the teacher to use the chalkboard and still maintain frequent viewing of the students in the classroom. The use of the chalkboard aids the visual learners in the class.

Outlining on the chalkboard or overhead is also an activity that effectively teaches visual learners, as it is both analytical (left brain) and spatial (right brain). A few additional rules that should be remembered in teaching to the visual learners in the classroom when using the chalkboard/overhead are:

- Keep it simple. Stick to key words and phrases. Do not clutter the chalkboard or the mind of the visual learner.
- Clean as you go. Once you finish a particular problem, example, or idea, clean the chalkboard. Do not cover the entire board only to need more space. This generally results in the

teacher cleaning a "hole" in the center of the board and writing in the newly cleaned area.

- Regardless of whether you are using a chalkboard/whiteboard, overhead, or computer, think of the visualization! What do you want the visual learner to see in their mind? Complete chaos from a disorganized chalkboard presentation, or a clear, organized visual presentation? Your use of the chalkboard will have an impact upon the visual learner. That impact will be either negative or positive, depending upon your level of organization. The use of a chalkboard, overhead, or PowerPoint cannot be haphazard.
- Positioning is important. The following examples have different meanings:

Lincoln   Washington

and

Lincoln
Washington

The first example implies that Washington and Lincoln are equal. The latter implies that either Lincoln was more important than Washington or that Lincoln preceded Washington. The placement of these two names on the chalkboard provides a definite implication to the students. By changing the placement, you change the implication. When writing on the chalkboard, the teacher needs to be aware of the importance of placement, and the resulting possible inferences that the placement may prompt in the minds of the visual learners.

Correct use of the chalkboard or overhead does require planning. Again, it is not haphazard. An effective classroom teacher is constantly aware of the visualization that is being created by the picture he or she is creating on the chalkboard or overhead.

Color also appears to have an impact on this visual picture. If there are particular items, words, and so on that you wish your students to remember, change from the basic color (white on a chalkboard, yellow on a whiteboard, black on the overhead) to red. In the same manner, if you make an error on the chalkboard or overhead, correct it in color. The students will remember the corrected item, not the error.

REVIEW: CLASSROOM MANAGEMENT TIPS TO REMEMBER

- Plan for the first day.
- Post clear classroom rules.
- Enforce all building rules.
- Treat all students with respect and dignity.
- Be consistent with classroom discipline.
- Use visual and verbal signals to correct off-task students.
- Assign consistent consequences for inappropriate behavior.
- Communicate with parents.
- Make effective use of the entire class period.
- Reduce student lag time.
- Always position yourself where you can see the entire class.
- During "seatwork," monitor the work of each student. Do not sit at your desk.
- Do not allow students to congregate in front of your desk or at the door.
- Write and submit disciplinary referrals for any student sent out of class.

SAMPLE CLASSROOM RULES

- Be on time.
- Raise your hand to ask or answer a question.
- The class ends when the teacher dismisses you.
- Know that we allow only one bathroom pass at a time.
- Treat each other with respect.

Explain each rule and give your rationale!

SAMPLE CLASS AGENDA: HIGH SCHOOL
SOCIAL STUDIES

- Write in your notebook what you believe are the major generalizations from World War I. (Note: This is a sponge activity.)
- Review the major effects of World War I.
- Describe the impact of the Treaty of Versailles on Germany.
- In your teams: Write about the inherent weaknesses of the Treaty of Versailles.
- Closure. (Closure will be discussed in chapter 2.)

SAMPLE CLASS AGENDA: MIDDLE SCHOOL ENGLISH LANGUAGE ARTS

- List the characteristics of a simile and a metaphor.
- Review some of the similes and metaphors from yesterday's reading.
- Identify the characteristics of personification.
- Identify the examples of personification in today's poem.
- Distinguish between a simile, a metaphor, and personification.
- Write a short poem containing examples of personification.

SAMPLE CLASS AGENDA: ELEMENTARY SCHOOL MATHEMATICS

- Write down the characteristics of a right triangle.
- Review the characteristics of a right triangle.
- Define isosceles triangle.
- Identify the characteristics of an isosceles triangle.
- Distinguish between an isosceles triangle and a right triangle.
- Draw and label a right and an isosceles triangle.

2

FOUR ESSENTIAL COMPONENTS

Without an appropriate climate created by effective classroom management techniques, learning cannot take place. The quality of that learning is indicative of the knowledge and effective use of "master teaching" techniques that have been documented by research for several years. Classes taught by the most effective classroom teachers contain the following four essential components:

- An initial sponge activity.
- A statement of the lesson's objective(s).
- Frequent checks to ensure student understanding.
- Closure at the end of the period.

SPONGE ACTIVITY

During the 1980s, Dr. Madeline Hunter identified seven components of lesson design. The first component of the lesson was termed the "anticipatory set." A sponge activity is virtually synonymous with the term "anticipatory set" (Russell 1987).

Dr. Hunter's recommendations were educationally sound and based upon a wealth of research on "effective teaching" techniques. The teachers' associations in some states did not always accept her teachings, due primarily to the fact that some building administrators misused these teachings. Building administrators were frequently directed to incorporate the seven elements of lesson design into the evaluation process but were not provided with either the time or funds necessary for adequate training. In countless districts, this resulted in simple checklists; each component was checked off if the supervisor observed it. Neutral terms such as "sponge activity" became substitutes for "anticipatory set" to avoid any negative connotations. Sponge activities are planned for the beginning of a class period, and are designed to maximize the amount of time on task. A sponge activity on the chalkboard/overhead when the students arrive serves to immediately:

- Focus the students mentally on the lesson.
- Motivate the students.
- Catch the students' covert (thinking) and overt (seated and quiet) attention.

An effective sponge activity actively involves the learner. It must relate to past, present, or future learning, and be relevant to the lessons' objectives (Russell 1987). Examples of appropriate sponge activities are:

- Answering released questions from state tests. All states have adopted statewide tests in English language arts and mathematics, with science and other tests to follow. Test questions from previous tests are released to schools annually. The released test questions serve as an excellent sponge activity daily throughout the school year in preparation for the tests.

- Identifying major points from previously learned material. As an example, if the previous day's lesson was an introduction to the English poets of the Romantic period, as the students enter the class, "In your notebook list the main characteristics of the poetry of the Romantic period" is on the chalkboard/overhead.
- Citing key points from the previous day's reading assignment. As an example, if by this time you have familiarized your students with the term "critical attributes" (to be discussed in a later chapter), "List the critical attributes of: simile, metaphor, and alliteration" is written on the chalkboard/overhead when the students enter the room.

A successful teacher effectively uses a sponge activity to provide students with a meaningful and relevant educational experience in the opening three to five minutes of each class. The students quickly learn to expect each class to begin in this manner, and look for the sponge activity when they enter the room.

A less-than-successful teacher virtually wastes these three to five minutes at the beginning of the class period each day, as the students are off task while the teacher takes roll and returns papers. Three to five minutes a day over the course of the school year equals nine to fifteen hours of instruction. With the use of sponge activities, these nine to fifteen hours of instructional time can become productive rather than wasted hours. A 2004 study based upon 1,500 classroom observations cited *zero percent* evidence of bell-to-bell instruction in the observations (Reeves 2005). Zero percent in 1,500 classroom observations! Consider the number of wasted instructional hours! Even though, as teachers, we know the value of time on task and the amount of time lost according to research, in practice we do not make appropriate use of the classroom time available. Every successful teacher teaches from bell to bell. They begin their classes with a sponge activity and use closure (explained later in this chapter) during the last few minutes to make sure that the students do understand and have achieved the objective. Compare this to allowing the students to talk and gather at the door for the final three minutes of the period. Also, as a classroom teacher, you do not want one of your building administrators to walk past your room before the bells rings and see your class piled up in front of the door waiting for the bell to ring!

Consider the following two scenarios: an effective mathematics teacher uses sponge activities daily to practice with released test questions from the state mathematics test, and another mathematics teacher wastes three to five minutes daily. At the end of the year, which students are more likely to be successful on the state mathematics test?

STATEMENT OF THE OBJECTIVE(S)

A statement of the objective identifies the specific behavior that is expected of the student. Surprisingly, some of the most effective teaching that I have witnessed personally took place in the U.S. Army. Every class began with a similar statement: "I am Sergeant So-and-so. I will be your principal instructor for the next ____ hours. At the end of this block of instruction, you will be able to ____" (for example, field strip, clean, and reassemble an M-14 rifle). Every student knew precisely what he or she had to be able to do at the conclusion of the instruction. There was no doubt. No one was required to guess what he or she would be expected to do at the end of the lesson.

In contrast, many classroom teachers merely inform their classes that "Today we are going to talk about World War II" or "about volcanoes." Generally, either example translates as "I'll talk and you will listen." In either of these scenarios, what will the students be required to do? What knowledge must they demonstrate? Will they be expected to state the date that the United States entered World War II? Will they be expected to describe the complex causes that led to World War II? Will they be asked to explain the American strategy for winning the war in the Pacific front? Or is the answer "all of the above"?

The same questions exist pertaining to the lesson on volcanoes. What knowledge will the students be required to demonstrate? Will they be asked to identify the critical attributes of a volcanic cone? Will they be asked to list a number of countries where active volcanoes can be found? Will they be asked to explain the role that volcanoes play in the formation of landforms?

The students have no way at all of determining what they must be able to do in order to be successful. There is absolutely no way of determining either the manner in which they must demonstrate the knowledge or the specific nature of the knowledge that they will have to demonstrate. Why would any teacher want this information to be a secret that is not to be shared with the students? Surprisingly, a 2004 study based upon 1,500 classroom observations indicated that a clear learning objective was observed in only 4 percent of the classes (Reeves 2005). Apparently, the students were left to guess what they were supposed to learn in the other 96 percent of the classes! The fact that a high percentage of teachers are not presenting their students with clear objectives is alarming. Classroom teachers, especially at the middle and high school levels, tend to be material oriented. They teach material rather than share objectives. In general, we learned to teach the way we ourselves were taught. We model the behavior of those who taught us. In doing this, we are ignoring what over two decades of research describes as the best practices. We must become familiar with the research, learn from it, and recognize that successful teachers follow these practices to increase student achievement.

Examples of proper objectives:

- The learner will be able to describe the various complex causes of World War II.
- The learner will be able to explain the American strategy for winning the war in the Pacific.
- The learner will be able to describe the various types of lava flows.
- The learner will be able to explain the critical attributes of a sonnet.
- The learner will distinguish between sedimentary and igneous rocks.
- The learner will identify angles as acute, right, or obtuse.

The objective must describe both the content to be learned and the activity (behavior). The activity must be measurable and observable. Often, objectives incorrectly include words such as

- Appreciate
- Enjoy
- Understand

Neither "appreciate" nor "enjoy" is measurable. "Understand" is too vague—how is the student to demonstrate that he or she understands? The specific activity used to measure the understanding needs to be written into the objective in place of "understand."

Begin by reviewing the unit that you will be teaching. What do you want the students to be able to do at the end of the unit? What knowledge do you want them to demonstrate? Take these unit objectives and break them down into daily lessons. On a day-by-day basis, what are the objectives for each lesson? What should the students know, demonstrate, or be able to do at the end of each lesson? Start with the "big picture" and work backward.

Not all teachers are comfortable writing objective(s) on the chalkboard or overhead. Nor are they comfortable writing "The learner/ student will." Neither is a necessity! These words may be omitted. The important factor is that the students be informed of the specific activity that they will be required to successfully perform to demonstrate their mastery of the objective(s).

One suggestion is to include the desired behavior in the posted agenda for the period—for example, "Describe the various complex causes of World War II."

Throughout the first weeks of school the teacher should explain that this portion of the lesson agenda clearly states the activity that the students will do to demonstrate mastery of the objective.

When constructing an objective, the choice of verb is critical. These verbs are categories according to the six levels of Bloom's taxonomy.

Knowledge

The student recalls specific information (Stevenson, Berner, and Brust 2001).

tell	name	touch
list	offer	write
cite	omit	underline
choose	pick	point out
arrange	quote	tally
find	repeat	transfer
group	say	underline
label	copy	recite
identify	locate	match

For example, you might design an objective requiring the learner to:

- Recite the poem "To Althea from Prison."
- Write the mathematical formula for solving polynomial equations.
- Identify the critical attributes of sedimentary rocks.

Comprehension

The student communicates an idea in a different form, sees the relationships among things, or imagines the effects of specific actions (Stevenson, Berner, and Brust 2001).

translate	infer	project
change	define	propose
construct	explain	advance
retell	outline	contemplate
qualify	annotate	paraphrase
convert	compare	contrast

For example, you might design an objective requiring the learner to:

- Rewrite the Declaration of Independence.
- Explain the meaning of President Woodrow Wilson's "Fourteen Points."
- Offer ways in which history might have been changed if President Lincoln had not been assassinated.
- Compare the structures and shapes of the different types of lava flows.
- Compare the characteristics of differently shaped polygons.

Application

The student uses the knowledge that he or she has acquired to find solutions to problems (Stevenson, Berner, and Brust 2001).

change	classify	dramatize
relate	utilize	solve
adopt	employ	use
exploit	try	prepare
operate	manipulate	practice

For example, you might design an objective requiring the learner to:

- Utilize your knowledge of formulas to calculate the square feet of the floor in this classroom and the cost of carpeting the room based upon $21.72 per square foot.
- Use the computer to write an essay demonstrating the keyboarding skills from the last lesson.

Analysis

The student uses the knowledge to separate information into component parts or characteristics (Stevenson, Berner, and Brust 2001).

break down	analyze	differentiate
dissect	take apart	deduce
assay	search	screen
inventory	examine	relate

For example, you might design an objective requiring the learner to:

- Search a particular painting for as many principles of art as possible.
- Analyze a compound for its specific elements.
- Take apart an object such as a microwave.

Synthesis

The student solves a problem by putting information together through original, creative thinking (Stevenson, Berner, and Brust 2001).

create	build	compile
compose	design	plan
produce	generate	develop
combine	make up	form

For example, you might design an objective requiring the learner to:

- Create a new national anthem.
- Develop a new way to teach the mathematical concept of "area."
- Generate a constitution for a newly independent country.
- Produce a study guide for the chapter.

Evaluation

The student makes qualitative and quantitative judgments according to set standards (Stevenson, Berner, and Brust 2001).

judge	rate	decide
evaluate	value	score
rank	determine	assess
award	choose	select

For example, you might design an objective requiring the learner to:

- Rank each of President Wilson's "Fourteen Points" in order of importance to you and describe why you chose this ranking.
- Decide which of the poems written by students in the class best match the characteristics of those written by the poets of the Romantic period.
- Score each of the students' paintings based upon established criteria.
- Determine the validity of an Internet source using set criteria.

Generally, as teachers, we focus too much on questions in class and on quizzes and tests that rely on the lower levels of Bloom's taxonomy (knowledge, comprehension, and application). We have an obligation to ensure that we are challenging students with higher level questions (analysis, synthesis, and evaluation). We must be teaching students to think rather than merely recall and apply information.

CHECK FOR UNDERSTANDING

The third essential component of any lesson is to check for understanding. Up to this point, an effective teacher's lesson has begun with a sponge activity that:

- Actively engaged all learners
- Maximized time on task
- Related to the objective

The effective teacher has also presented a clear and measurable objective that has identified the

- Content
- Behavior to be exhibited

Throughout the balance of the lesson, it is critical that the teacher continually measure the level of the students' understanding. How will we know that the students are learning? Regardless of the methodology employed (for example, lecture, discussion, cooperative learning, project work, etc.), the teacher must be certain that all students comprehend the material and exhibit the skills required to meet the objective. In other words, throughout the period, an effective teacher will continually

Assess   Assess   Assess   Assess   Assess

Assessment, as defined by Spence Rogers, is "the gathering of information in order to change our [the teacher's] behavior to improve performance." This is in contrast to evaluation, which Spence Rogers defines as being "scored or graded." Assessment is a critical part of the teaching process (Rogers 2005). Madeline Hunter referred to this as "checking for understanding" as you teach. If the assessment indicates that the students do not understand the material, the teacher backs up and reteaches. For example, if the students did not understand the procedure to solve a mathematics problem, the teacher presents a different explanation, rather than *repeating* the same explanation again. The heart of teaching almost any subject, but especially mathematics, is to be able to provide a second and third explanation for students who did not understand the first one. Successful teachers will also ask the class if one of the students would care to present an explanation in his or her own words.

Some ways in which an effective teacher checks the students' level of understanding throughout the lesson are:

- Directed questions
- Signals
- Silent response

Directed Questions

Directed questions are those questions for which specific students are called upon to answer, as opposed to "choral" questions, which are tossed out to the entire class and *no specific student* is called upon for an answer. One student or several may yell out an answer to a choral question. In terms of determining whether the students understand the material, choral questions are useless.

Some typical questions that could be either choral or directed:

- Who can tell me the first step in solving this equation?
- What is the correct present-tense form of this "-ar" verb in Spanish?
- Who can tell me how "buying on margin" helped cause the Crash of 1929?
- Who can give me an example of alliteration in today's reading?
- Who can explain the difference between an anticline and a syncline?
- Who can tell me the time if I move the big hand from the three to the nine?

Most of the examples cited above can involve multiple students. Different students can be called upon for each of the remaining steps in solving the equation, other forms of the "-ar" verb, or additional examples of alliteration from the reading assignment. An effective teacher will check the level of understanding among several students with each question.

One major point to remember when asking questions is that *it is most effective* to present the question first, wait, and then call upon a student for the answer.

If a teacher says, "John, what is the first step in solving this equation?" John is the only one thinking; the rest of the class knows that

John is the only one on the spot. An effective teacher will say, "I will ask someone to tell me the first step." The effective teacher will pause, providing some wait time (wait time will be discussed in more detail later), and make eye contact with several students, creating the belief that anyone in the class may be called upon. All students should know that they are accountable!

A second major point to remember when asking questions is to remember that an effective teacher checks the level of understanding of as many different students as possible during the period, and among students of all ability levels. The objective for the teacher is to ensure that the *class*, not just a handful of students, can demonstrate their achievement of the lesson's objective.

A less-than-successful teacher employs choral questions or allows a few brighter students to answer all questions. In either case, such a teacher has no idea of the level of understanding among most of the students in the class.

A third major point to remember is that the effective classroom teacher provides adequate wait time following a question before calling upon a student for a response. Research by Mary Budd Rowe indicated that the average wait time by a classroom teacher was a mere one second (Ellis and Worthington 1994).

The same study showed that with an adequate wait time (thirty seconds):

- The length of student responses increased.
- The number of volunteers increased.
- The failure to respond decreased.

The conclusion was that the strategy providing adequate wait time increased student thinking. Thirty seconds can seem more like five minutes to the teacher, but the thirty-second wait time is effective! It is also effective for the teacher to rephrase the question during this wait time.

Successful teachers assess constantly throughout the lesson. They also use questions to promote retention and transfer by reinforcing the learning through their responses to the students' correct answers.

At worst, a less-than-effective teacher ignores a correct answer from a student and continues with the lesson; at best, he or she provides the individual student who answered the question correctly with positive reinforcement by acknowledging that the answer is correct. A successful teacher, however, acknowledges the correct answer and repeats it for the class to again hear in the language of the original learning (not necessarily the words that the student used in answering correctly). The repetition reinforces and strengthens the learning, increasing the probability of retention and the ability to transfer (apply) the learning.

The above is one variable in both retention and transfer (to be discussed later); another variable is the degree of original learning. Simply stated, the stronger the original learning, the greater the probability of retention and transfer. As an example, the teacher has taught the class to differentiate between stalagmites and stalactites by saying "stalac*tites* stick *tight* to the ceiling." When asked to differentiate, a correct student response may have included this original phrase, or simply "stalagmites rise from the floor while stalactites hang from the ceiling." Either way, the successful teacher would respond with "Very good. Stalactites stick tight to the ceiling." Again, this repetition of the original learning provides reinforcement, strengthens the degree of original learning, and thereby promotes retention and transfer.

Signals

Signals are a method by which a teacher may visually assess the understanding of an entire class at one time. Frequently this is done with "thumbs up if . . ." and "thumbs down if. . . ." Although some high school teachers are reluctant to use this method, as they believe it more appropriate for lower levels, high school students accept it, as do students in master's degree programs!

A method that provides more flexibility is to use one, two, three, or four fingers to respond. An example of this method is when the teacher writes on the chalkboard or on the overhead

1 = Simile
2 = Metaphor
3 = Personification
4 = Alliteration

As the teacher reads various examples of these literary devices, the students are asked to indicate their classification by a show of fingers. The teacher can visually see the level to which each literary device is understood by the class. It is a much more efficient use of time than calling upon a different student for each of the examples.

Of course, if this assessment indicates that students do not clearly understand "personification," the teacher reteaches that literary device before moving on. A successful teacher understands that it is much better to teach half of the curriculum and have it thoroughly understood than to teach the entire curriculum without an understanding by the students. The students need to understand the material! Merely focusing on covering everything does not provide for the students' understanding of the information. In the latter case, there is no mastery of the objectives, no retention or transfer, and no preparation for future course work. Emphasis has to be placed on mastering the objective, ensuring the ability to retain and transfer the knowledge, and the preparation for future learning.

Less-than-effective teachers believe, and occasionally verbalize, the fact that they "put it out there; if the students do not get it, it's their problem." Wrong. It is the teacher's problem. Did that teacher assess, assess, assess, and assess? No. A successful teacher assesses student understanding throughout the lesson; if the understanding is not there, the teacher reteaches.

Silent Response

It is essential that assessment also occur through silent responses during student seatwork, whether the seatwork is done individually or in teams or groups. An effective teacher moves from student/group to student/group to assess and assist. A less-than-effective teacher will sit at his or her desk, grading papers; this is synonymous with placing a large sign on the desk stating "Don't Bother Me."

No teacher can spend four or five minutes assessing or assisting each student during seatwork. Do the math. In a class of sixteen students, how many can you reach during a twenty-minute span? Are all of the students in the class on task during the five minutes a teacher works with one student?

One effective strategy to use is "Praise. Prompt. Leave." This strategy enables the master teacher to spend thirty seconds assessing and assisting each student. Rosenshine reported that teacher contacts with students doing independent work should be limited to thirty seconds (Ellis and Worthington 1994).

Always give clues in the prompt. Do not tell the student the answer. By employing this strategy, a successful teacher is able to assess and assist every student in the class, even returning a second time to the student(s) who was stalled on step two of the problem.

John Collins's "Type One" writing can be an effective means of monitoring at any point in a teacher's lesson. In his Type One writing, volume is stressed (Collins 2005). The literature teacher, for example, would ask the students to "write down ten examples of personification; you have two and one-half minutes." Precisely

Praise.	Provide the student with honest positive reinforcement. "You have done the first step correctly. Nice job." Do not say "but . . . " It cancels the positive reinforcement.
Prompt.	Determine where the student is stalled and provide a clue. "Look at the steps again. Follow step two and I will return."
Leave.	Do not stay to watch the student work through step two. Move to the next student. You will come back again to check on the student, but you must move on to get to others. You cannot end up spending five or ten minutes with one student at the expense of the others.

two and one-half minutes later, the teacher can (1) pair students, or (2) collect some as a random quiz (such as every third or fourth student's list). All papers should be viewed by the teacher to measure understanding. Type One writing is graded on a check or minus basis. If the teacher asked for ten examples, papers meeting the criteria are given a check. Obviously, monitoring is but one of many uses for Type One writing.

The same 2004 study based upon 1,500 classroom observations that highlighted the low percentage of teachers who provided students with a clear objective also indicated an alarming statistic regarding monitoring. In 22 percent of the classrooms observed, monitoring took place without any feedback provided to the student (Reeves 2005).

What is the effectiveness of monitoring, if no feedback is given? Many teachers believe that saying "Good job" is providing meaningful feedback to a student. Do not confuse feedback with praise or positive reinforcement. "Good job" is praise or positive reinforcement; it is *not* feedback. Grant Wiggins defines feedback as "reporting on what the student did against a specific target (objective)—no personal value or aesthetic judgment is made." Grant Wiggins states that feedback is descriptive, not evaluative; it is not praise or blame, nor is it guidance or advice (Wiggins 2005). Two example of feedback are:

- Good job! You have identified two metaphors in the paragraph. Can you locate one more?
- Very good work. You have worked the first two steps in the math problem correctly. Review for me the third step in solving this type of problem.

CLOSURE

Now, we come to the end of the period and closure. Closure is *not* the teacher summarizing the learning and telling the students that "Today you learned that . . ." Closure *is* the teacher asking diagnostic questions to determine if the students have mastered the objective. Kindsvatter, Wilen, and Ishler (1988) described proper closure as reinforcing the learners' lesson.

Look at your objective(s) for the lesson; what questions do you need to ask to determine if your objectives were met? If your objective was to have the students explain simile and metaphor and distinguish between them, your diagnostic closure questions might be:

- Who can define simile for me?
- Who can give me two examples of a simile?
- Who can define metaphor for me?

- Who can give me two examples of a metaphor?
- Who can draw both a digital clock and a clock with hands to show me the time nine fifteen? How about ten forty-five? And eleven fifty-five?

In each case, after providing appropriate wait time, the teacher should call upon specific students for the answers. As one final step in providing closure, the teacher might show several similes and metaphors on the chalkboard/overhead or in a PowerPoint and ask that several students identify each one as a simile or a metaphor—and explain the reason for their answers.

Closure:

- Maintains focus at the end of the period, maximizing time on task.
- Is planned in advance, not at the end of the period.
- Is more difficult to do well than a sponge activity.

REVIEW: FOUR ESSENTIALS TO REMEMBER

- Initial sponge activity
  Focuses the students on the lesson
  Motivates the students
  Acquires the students' covert and overt attention
  Maximizes time on task
- Statement of the objective
  Describes both the content and the activity
  The activity must be measurable
  Post the objective
- Check for understanding
  Direct questions to individual or multiple students
  Present the question before calling upon the student
  Use wait-pause strategy
  Reinforce the original learning with repetition
  Use signal responses to measure the entire class
  Reteach when understanding is not present
  Use praise-prompt-leave to assess seatwork
  Closure maintains focus at the end of the period

REVIEW: SPONGE ACTIVITIES

- Focus students on the subject matter
- Provide for practice/review, application, and transfer
- Are only three to five minutes in length
- Assist in classroom management
- Are meaningful activities that prevent wasted time

3

TEACHING TO
THE OBJECTIVE

L ook again at the example of the teaching in the U.S. Army: "At
the end of this block of instruction, you will be able to . . ."
Look at the other examples from chapter 2:

- The learner will describe the various complex causes of
  World War II.
- The learner will explain the American strategy for winning
  the war in the Pacific.
- The learner will describe the various types of lava flows.
- The learner will explain the critical attributes of a sonnet.
- The learner will distinguish between sedimentary and ig-
  neous rocks.
- The learner will identify angles as acute, right, or obtuse.

All of these examples are specific. They clearly identify what activity the learner will be able to perform. Research (for example,
Rosenshine 1986, as cited in Ellis and Worthington 1994) states
that two of the elements of effective teaching are:

- A clearly defined behavioral objective
- Maximum time on task

Student achievement is directly related to time on task. Simply stated, as the amount of time spent on task increases, so does student achievement. Obviously, you cannot spend an unlimited amount of time on each course objective. You can, however, utilize classroom time effectively and maximize the amount of time on task by focusing on teaching to the objective.

Madeline Hunter and Douglas Russell defined teaching to the objective as "Generating in the learner overt behaviors that are *relevant* to the learning, meaning producing observable and measurable behaviors that are pertinent to the learning" (Russell 1987).

To that definition, add *from bell to bell.* In other words, every minute of class time—from the beginning sponge activity to the closure lasting to the ending bell—is related to the objective. If we go back to our examples, every minute of class time from the beginning sponge activity through closure focuses entirely on:

- The learner will describe the various complex causes of World War II.
- The learner will explain the American strategy for winning the war in the Pacific.
- The learner will describe the various types of lava flows.
- The learner will explain the critical attributes of a sonnet.
- The learner will distinguish between sedimentary and igneous rocks.
- The learner will identify angles as acute, right, or obtuse.

The key word in Hunter and Russell's definition of teaching to the objective is *relevant.* All student behavior, regardless of the activity, must be relevant to the learning. To be relevant, this behavior is:

- Pertinent and necessary
- Efficient in the use of time
- Effective in producing achievement

Start with your objective(s). Ask yourself, "What is the best way to teach this?" Work backward from your objective(s). What activities meet the criteria listed above? Some of the most outstanding examples of this come from successful teachers in foreign language. In a French class, a teacher whose objective was for students to appropriately use a list of vocabulary words with accurate gender for nouns and tense for the verbs:

- Posted the related sponge activity on the overhead projector
- Divided the class into preassigned groups
- Directed each group through a different activity (wrote a restaurant menu, sang a song, performed a skit, created a poster)
- Established a common time limit for each activity
- Monitored and assisted each group
- Instructed each group to rotate to the next activity at the end of the set time
- Provided activities that related directly to the objective

In an example from an algebra class, the teacher posted several equations on the overhead projector when the class began. The teacher then:

- Divided the class into prearranged groups
- Monitored each group as they worked to solve all of the equations
- Moved the seats against the wall
- Instructed each group to graph their equation on the floor

- Had each group show their mathematical work on the chalk-board

In both examples, the student behavior was relevant to the learning. The behavior was:

- Pertinent and necessary
- Efficient in the use of time
- Effective in producing achievement

In both of these examples, the teacher closely monitored the student groups, constantly moving from group to group, listening and guiding. The "praise-prompt-leave" strategy explained in chapter 2 was employed to guide any group that experienced difficulty. The close monitoring of the groups ensured that all groups remained focused on the task. The "praise-prompt-leave" strategy permitted the teacher to visit each group several times.

The effect of the close monitoring is to:

- Make sure that students in each group are focused and on task
- Make sure that the work is correct

The latter is essential to prevent incorrect learning, such as a vocabulary or pronunciation error in the French class. Incorrect learning provides negative transfer in future learning, as well as the present.

As a classroom teacher, you have to plan the learning needed for the students to achieve the designed behavioral objective. This requires that you:

- Demonstrate the skills to be learned or explain the concept to be learned (modeling)

- Plan a variety of activities to meet the objective
- Monitor the level of student understanding

Some of the best teaching of skills can be viewed daily on school athletic fields or courts. Watch an athletic practice on any given day to see the teaching of skills. Any skill taught is:

- Demonstrated correctly
- Broken into parts
- Practiced part by part until each is mastered
- Practiced, practiced, and practiced

For an example of teaching a concept, refer to the one titled "Spiral" in chapter 4.

Research conducted by Edgar Dale in the 1960s was illustrated by a cone or pyramid. The tip of the cone or pyramid represented the least effective means of learning, showing that students remember only 10 percent of what they read. The cone/pyramid broadens out to 20 percent, as students remember 20 percent of what they hear. Reading *and* lecturing still only add up to a 30 percent retention rate, yet in most classrooms, this accounts for the vast majority of the teaching. We know that students learn more through active learning (doing).

Continuing down the cone/pyramid, Dale concluded that students remembered 30 percent of what they see (watch videos or view an exhibit, for example) and 50 percent of what they hear and see (such as a demonstration or field trip). The retention rate increases to 70 percent by involving the students in both speaking and writing (such as participating in a hands-on workshop). The base of the cone/pyramid indicates that the rate of retention by students increases to 90 percent of what they say and do (dramatized experiences, simulations, or presentations, for example) (Active Learning Team n.d.).

Why do some teachers continue to teach solely by lecturing when the retention rate is *only* 20 percent? In sharp contrast, we know that students remember 70 to 90 percent of what they learn through active learning techniques. Active learning is activity-based learning, as opposed to the passive learning of the students listening to a lecture. These activities may involve whole-class, team, or small-group participation. The activities can involve reading, speaking, writing, drawing, dramatizing, building, creating, and so forth (Active Learning Team n.d.).

The vast increase in computers in schools has enormously expanded the opportunities for active learning activities. Classroom teachers at all grade levels from elementary through high school are assigning computer work to their classes. Teachers who have at least one computer per four students in their classroom are far more likely to assign computer work than teachers with a higher ratio or those who use computer labs (Becker, Ravitz, and Wong 1999). The computer is not only useful in teaching keyboarding and word processing skills but also for research projects and PowerPoint demonstrations. It allows for collaborative learning and multimedia learning experiences.

The importance of monitoring student responses to measure their level of understanding cannot possibly be overstated. It was discussed in chapter 2 and will be examined again in more depth.

A successful teacher plans:

- Questions that match the objective
- Questions on various levels of Bloom's taxonomy
- Questions at regular three- to eight-minute intervals throughout the lesson

Effective questioning is not a spontaneous event. Specific questions and their location in the lesson are planned in advance. As with all elements of effective teaching, a considerable amount of research exists regarding the effectiveness of questions in class lessons.

Kindsvatter, Wilen, and Ishler (as cited in Ellis and Worthington 1994) found that teachers with well-planned and patterned sequences of questions appear to have had an improvement in student learning. They also reported that in some heterogeneously grouped classes, phrasing questions in simple, clear language increased the probability that all students would understand them. More thought-provoking questions should be included for the more advanced students. Kindsvatter, Wilen, and Ishler also found that student participation increased when teachers asked questions of nonvolunteers. They concluded that too often teachers relied on a few volunteering students. When *all* students are expected to contribute, student participation increases.

Sindelar, Bursuck, and Halle (as cited in Ellis and Worthington 1994) reported that ordered, predictable questions positively and significantly correlated with student achievement. Anderson (as cited in Ellis and Worthington 1994) found that calling on students in order (row-by-row, alphabetical, etc.) was most effective, and that calling on volunteers or students at random or accepting "called-out" responses was least effective. Brophy and Evertson (as cited in Ellis and Worthington 1994), however, found that accepting "called-out" responses from low achievers resulted in significant gains in achievement. Their conclusion was that any responses from low achievers improved student achievement.

We know that peer tutoring results in increased achievement for both the student doing the tutoring and the student who is being tutored (Ellis and Worthington 1994). Research by King (as cited in Ellis and Worthington 1994) shows that reciprocal peer questioning promotes student achievement through student-student interaction. Marksberry (as cited in Ellis and Worthington 1994) stated that teachers need to instruct students how to ask questions. Instruction should include proper form, uses, and limitations to the questions. Ellis and Lenz (1992) found that teachers gave low-achieving students fewer opportunities and less time in which to respond than they gave to average or high-achieving students.

Very little research has been conducted on the effectiveness of choral response (anyone or everyone responds) and its relationship to student achievement. The research that does exist is contradictory. Brophy and Evertson (as cited in Ellis and Worthington 1994) reported a negative relationship between choral responses and student achievement. The Oregon District Instruction Follow-Through program, however, found that choral responses had a positive impact upon student achievement (Ellis and Worthington 1994).

As a classroom teacher, ask yourself:

- If you permit choral questions, why?
- If you only call upon volunteering students, why?
- What does either indicate in terms of the number of students in the class who have achieved the stated objective?

The amount of research on questioning techniques is considerable. The most obvious fact from reviewing the research is that effective questions do not just happen. The questions are planned in advance. The placement of the questions throughout the lesson is planned rather than being an impromptu act.

Asking questions as well as planning effective questions is an art. Generally, there are three types of questions:

- Factual questions
- Interpretive questions
- Evaluative questions

Factual questions have one simple, correct answer. They are basic recall questions (Youth Learn Institute 2003):

- What is an anticline?
- What is a sonnet?
- What are the properties of a right triangle?
- What are the characteristics of a polynomial?

Interpretive questions have more than one answer and lead to follow-up questions requiring further information or support. The art of asking interpretive questions is to develop questions that build from one to another (Youth Learn Institute 2003):

- What was the major element in winning World War II? How did the Allied strategy support and utilize this element? How did this element change warfare?
- What do you believe our forefathers intended when they wrote the U.S. Constitution?
- What is an isosceles triangle? How does it differ from an equilateral triangle? By changing the angles, how many different types of triangles may be formed? What happens if you add a fourth side? Now how many figures can be formed?
- Whom do you consider to be the champion of the sonnet? How do his or her sonnets differ from those of other contemporary writers?
- What is an idiom? What are the characteristics of an idiom? What are some of the idioms you found in today's story? Who can give me some of your own examples of idioms?

Evaluative questions have no right or wrong answer as they call for an opinion or belief. They open the opportunity for discussion at the higher levels of Bloom's taxonomy (Youth Learn Institute 2003):

- Decide between the two menus; which is more nutritious? Why?
- Rate the following persuasive essays according to the strength of their respective cases. Explain your reasoning.
- Determine which of these two experiments provides more conclusive results. How did you come to that answer?

In addition to the levels of Bloom's taxonomy, questions may also be categorized according to their formulation (Drummond 2002):

- Description:
    What is the difference between these two clocks?
    What is the difference between these two poetry forms?
    What are the differences between these three types of rock?
- Common purpose or function:
    What is the function of the line judge?
    What is the purpose of a stethoscope?
    What is the purpose of using rubrics?
- Procedures:
    What is the next step in solving the equation?
    What is the next procedure in writing a sonnet?
    What is the next step in this experiment?
- Possibilities:
    What type of rock might this be?
    How could we change this simile into a metaphor?
    What other possible ways can we solve this mathematical problem?
- Prediction:
    What will happen if we add this chemical?
    If the barometer drops, what will be the likely effect on our weather?

If our heroine in the story did not do what she did, what would you think would have happened?

- Justification:

    What evidence led you to conclude the rock was metamorphic?

    Why do you believe that is the best way to solve the problem?

    How did you come to the conclusion that airpower led to the Allied victory?

- Generalization:

    What is the same about these two types of problems?

    How are these two landforms similar?

    What generalizations can you make about the types of warfare seen in World War I and World War II?

- Definition:

    What does totalitarian mean?

    What is an analog clock?

    What is a polynomial?

The most important fact to remember as a teacher is that all of the above questions should be followed with "Why?" or "Explain how you came to that conclusion/answer." Do not stop at simple answers; have the student explain his or her reasoning and the process or procedure that was used to arrive at the response.

All questions should relate to the objective. In checking for understanding, some questions at the lower end of Bloom's taxonomy (knowledge and comprehension) are a necessity. However, effective questions:

- Build on knowledge and comprehension levels of questions
- Indicate the students' ability to apply (transfer) the knowledge
- Require students to function at the analysis, synthesis, and evaluation levels

We also know that a pattern frequently exists in teacher-student interactions. Studies have concluded that generally a T-shape pattern can be found. The T shape is a result of teacher interactions with the students located across the front row and down the center of the classroom. Noticeably, teacher interactions are absent or less frequent with the students located in the rear rows and in both the left and right corners of the room.

It is suggested that a teacher ask a colleague, department chair, or administrator to sit in on his or her class and complete an interaction chart for the teacher's own use. This simply requires that a colleague, department chair, or administrator use a seating chart to map each teacher-student interaction. For each interaction, a tick mark is placed on the seating chart for the responding student. The teacher should review the chart, note the pattern, and consider why each of the interactions were directed to the specific students.

Finally, in teaching to the objective, when responding to student answers:

- Provide the student with positive reinforcement.
- Coach students who provide incorrect responses to reach success. Instead of providing the student with the correct answer, lead the student to the correct answer through a series of questions. After receiving an incorrect answer to a math problem, for example, take the student through the problem step-by-step so that the student will arrive at the correct answer after recognizing where the error was made.
- Repeat the students' responses in the original language of the learning. This reinforces and strengthens the degree of the original learning.

REVIEW: RESEARCH SHOWS IN TEACHING TO THE OBJECTIVE, YOU SHOULD

- Plan your questions in sequences
- Phrase questions in clear, simple language
- Plan questions at various levels of Bloom's taxonomy
- Ask questions of both nonvolunteering and volunteering students
- Plan some questions to be answered in a predictable order
- Avoid "called-out" responses except in homogeneous classes for lower-ability students
- Direct questions to students both in order and at random
- After training, use reciprocal peer questioning periodically
- Remember to ask questions of low-achieving students and give them adequate response time
- Have a sound rationale for accepting choral questions or only calling upon volunteering students

The Green Bay (Wisconsin) Area Public Schools created a document for their teachers that includes the following questions (among others):

Does the teacher:

- understand that all behaviors fostered by the teacher to aid the students in achieving the objective need to be relevant and/or pertinent to the objective?
- understand that all language used by the teacher and by the students needs to be specific, clear, and concise?
- understand that teaching to the objective is an instructional skill?
- understand that efficiency of time and effectiveness of learning are goals of a teacher in every lesson?
- understand that every lesson is a balance of efficiency of time and effectiveness of learning?
- understand that the student behaviors need to be observable and measurable?
- understand that teaching to the objective is the responsibility of the teacher and not the student?
- understand that, in providing specific and relevant activities for the student, the teacher is satisfying one of the requirements of teaching to the objective?
- understand that, in responding to the students' answers to questions in the language of the original learning, the teacher is satisfying another requirement of teaching to the objective?
- understand that, by asking questions, the teacher is measuring the level of student understanding?
- understand that several relevant questions need to be asked of many students to determine the level of student understanding?

- understand that the statement of the objective should be clear, concise, and specific, indicating the expected learning behavior?

To this, it is recommended that we add:

- understand that activities involving active learning should be included in the lesson?
- understand that, depending upon the length of the class period, three to six activities should be planned? Plan on each activity taking fifteen minutes, or three activities for a forty-five-minute period, six activities for an eighty- to ninety-minute block.
- understand that questions need to be planned in advance?

REVIEW: TO TEACH TO THE OBJECTIVE

- Write a clearly defined behavioral objective stating the observable and measurable outcome
- Plan a related sponge activity
- Plan an appropriate number of student activities for the length of the class
- Plan some activities for active learning
- Review the activities for efficiency of time and effectiveness of learning
- Closely monitor student activities to focus and ensure correct learning
- Plan questions relevant to the objective at various levels of Bloom's taxonomy
- Plan for questions to be asked at a frequency rate of every three to eight minutes
- Apply the knowledge learned through research on questioning
- Plan for closure

4

TEACHING
FOR RETENTION

Do you remember the word FOIL from the algebra class that you had in high school?

First
Outers
Inners
Last

What about this sentence from your middle school science class?

My
Very
Energetic
Mother
Just
Served
Us
Nine
Pizzas

The latter, of course, stands for the nine planets in their order from the sun (Mercury, Venus, Earth, Mars, Jupiter, Saturn, Uranus, Neptune, and Pluto).

Other examples are the lines and spaces that you memorized in music class, *Every Good Boy Does Fine* (lines) and *FACE* (the spaces). Many of us still use *HOMES* any time we wish to recall the names of the Great Lakes.

In each of these examples, a first letter was taken from a word to either spell another word (FOIL, HOMES) or to make words that form a sentence. This process is called a mnemonic device and assists in increasing retention by adding meaning. Even in the electronic age and at a time when teaching students to be "lifelong learners" is emphasized, mnemonic devices are important because retention is still important! Math teachers still use FOIL.

Meaning is the most important factor in fostering increased retention. As a teacher, you want to increase the probability of your students retaining knowledge in their long-term memory. To do this:

- Identify the concept or skill that you want to be retained
- Work with the information to create a mnemonic device to provide meaning

Examples are another powerful force in increasing the probability of long-term retention. Because of the power of examples, care must be taken in selecting them. It is better to think "on your seat, instead of your feet." You cannot plan your examples while walking from the school parking lot to your classroom. To be effective, examples must:

- Be clear
- Be relevant to the students' own lives

- Be planned in advance
- Be free from ambiguity or distractions (controversy or emotion)

Here is an example from a teacher's lesson combining a mnemonic device reinforced with examples relevant to the students' daily lives. The teacher wanted to increase the probability of the six causes of the Great Depression of 1929 being retained in the students' long-term memory.

Easy money
Unequal distribution of income
Weak bank structure
Inflated stock prices
Unstable corporate structure
Pessimistic attitude

The teacher rephrased the six weaknesses to create a mnemonic device (the word SPIRAL) and examples were planned that added meaning, increased interest, and utilized similarities. The six weaknesses were presented by the teacher, who wrote in color:

S
P
I
R
A
L

Each of the six weaknesses was introduced and explained separately, along with student-centered examples. One by one, the meaning of the acronym was unveiled by writing the rephrased weakness in another color next to the letter. The level of the students' understanding was monitored and reinforced prior to the introduction of the next weakness. The monitoring measured both the students' recall of the term presented for the weakness and their knowledge of its meaning. A variety of monitoring techniques was used, including signaling, one-to-one verbal responses, one-to-multiple verbal responses (in which the teacher calls on several students, each of whom answers a different part of a larger question), and written responses. The key here is that each of the weaknesses was taught, mastered, and reinforced before the next weakness was introduced.

The rephrased weaknesses and the examples that were introduced are:

S = Structure of corporations

The pyramiding of corporations was shown to be similar to a pyramid constructed by ten cheerleaders (four-person base, three on the second tier, etc.). Both of the pyramids fall if a cheerleader—or a company—in the base collapses. The concept of a cheerleader pyramid is very familiar to the students; it is a concept that is relevant to their own lives.

P = Pessimism

The attitude of the American people during the months preceding the crash of 1929 was compared to the attitude of a student toward taking a difficult exam when, despite honorable intentions, he or she has not studied. If time is eventually available in the last hours before the exam, it is perceived as being too late to avoid the inevitable. The student is aware that the results of the test will be bad and there is nothing that can be done to alter the outcome. The student's feeling of pessimism is similar to that felt by the American people in 1929: "It is going to be bad, and there is nothing that can be done."

I = Inflated stock prices

After the initial explanation, the teacher asked one student requiring motivation if he or she would give the teacher $3,000 for the teacher's ten-year-old Ford van. When the student declined, the teacher asked if the student would buy the van for $3,000 if she could resell it to another student for $3,500. This example continued with other students purchasing and reselling the van until the purchase price had reached $6,000. At this point, the class was asked to determine the fair market value of the vehicle and compare that value to the last amount paid.

The class was then asked what the effect was on the last purchaser, and then explained the phenomena that caused the price to rise. The sale of the van was similar to conditions in the stock market from 1927 to 1929, when prices became inflated by 300 percent due to speculation. In both cases, the speculation could not continue indefinitely.

R = "Runs" on banks

The concept of a run on banks was compared to an announced sale at school during the noon hour of tickets for a popular rock star's concert. If only a very limited number of tickets were found to be available, what would the effect be if another ticket sale were announced the following day? The resulting and inevitable run on the concert tickets would be similar to a run on the banks during the Depression. The shortage of funds (like the shortage of tickets) would cause a run on other banks.

A = All unequal distribution of income

The explanation was given that a mere 5 percent of the population of the United States controlled an exceptionally large percentage of the money supply after World War I. This small percentage of the population increased its share of the money supply during the prosperous 1920s. For the bulk of the American population, the supply of money did not keep pace with inflation through the decade. The buying power of the American population declined drastically.

The example provided was that of a student's allowance (or salary) staying the same throughout high school despite prices on items (such as CDs) doubling each year. The student's ability to buy such items would drop at a drastic rate over the four years of high school.

L = Loose (easy) money

The Federal Reserve failed to raise the interest rate to tighten the money supply during the late 1920s. The similarity of the money supply to an individual's diet was presented by the teacher. In times of prosperity, it is healthy to tighten up on one's diet. In the case of the late 1920s, the Federal Reserve allowed the country to "pig out."

After completing the explanations and examples for each of the six weaknesses, the teacher removed all of the written weaknesses, leaving only:

S
P
I
R
A
L

For visual emphasis, the teacher added a graphic to the left of the letters that resembled a tornado—a visual, downward spiral. The visualization was further expanded by adding underneath:

Downward spiral in economy = Depression

For closure, the students were directed to turn to empty pages in their notebooks, copy down the letters, and enter the six terms after the six letters, along with a brief explanation of each weakness. During this exercise, the teacher moved throughout the room, monitoring the work of each student.

You will note that in the above example:

- A mnemonic device was employed
- The six weaknesses were presented separately
- The level of understanding was measured after each weakness
- The examples related to the students' daily lives
- The students were left with a visualization of a downward spiral

All of the above required planning. The teacher began by first determining what concept was to be retained in the students' long-term memory. The teacher then worked out a mnemonic device and meaningful examples to increase the probability of retention. In the final steps of preparing the lesson, the teacher referred to the research on effective teaching, separated the six weaknesses, added planned questions to measure the level of understanding after each weakness, and decided how visual emphasis could be added to assist the visual learners.

The human brain has a limited storage capacity for short-term memory; generally this is considered to be seven items. Items are stored first in the short-term memory, prior to storage in the unlimited capacity of long-term memory. When going beyond seven items, such as a list of nine planets, it is best to either use a mnemonic device or break the nine items down into smaller units.

An example from a high school health class unit on blood pressure listed the following factors: weight, age, rate of heartbeat, exercise, emotion, eating habits, volume, vessel, and viscosity.

The teacher divided the above into three groups of three (Hunter 1987):

3 Vs—volume, vessel, viscosity
WAR—weight, age, rate
3 Es—exercise, emotion, eating

Again, as in the history class, the teacher employed examples from the students' daily lives when presenting each of the above factors affecting blood pressure. Again, the teacher presented each of the nine factors separately and checked the level of understanding on each before moving to the next factor. Again, the teacher included visualizations as part of the lesson.

The history teacher and the health teacher created these lessons with the deliberate intent of improving the students' long-term retention of the material. A mnemonic device worksheet follows, which will help guide you in determining your own lesson.

MNEMONIC DEVICE WORKSHEET

Activity: _____

List a concept or skill from your current lesson that you want retained.

Develop a mnemonic device for this concept or skill.

Develop examples that relate to your students' daily lives.

5

TEACHING
FOR TRANSFER

It should be noted that this chapter relies heavily on material presented in classes taught by Madeline Hunter and Doug Russell at the University of Wisconsin–Green Bay. Transfer is the process of a student's past learning influencing future learning. It is the heart of excellent teaching, as it is the ability of students to apply classroom learning to future situations that arise, both in school and in life. Problem solving in life requires transfer (Hunter 1987).

Given the above definition, it is easy to comprehend the importance of transfer. We want students to be able to apply what they learn—later in the course, in future courses, and in daily situations, now and in the future. This ability to apply learning cannot be left to mere chance. In order for transfer to occur, the teacher must have a knowledge of the factors that influence transfer; these factors increase the probability that the student will be able to apply what has been taught.

Transfer is essential for:

- faster learning
- critical thinking
- problem solving
- reasoning

Transfer is required to apply material from the knowledge and comprehension levels of Bloom's taxonomy to application, analysis, synthesis, and evaluation (see the following transfer worksheet). Grant Wiggins states that students really understand when they can: explain, interpret, apply, adapt, see from a different perspective, show empathy, and reveal self-understanding (Wiggins 2005). Transfer, then, constitutes proof that the students have learned.

Transfer that aids in the acquisition of new learning is referred to as positive transfer. Transfer that deters or slows the acquisition of new learning is referred to as negative transfer. One of the best examples highlighting positive and negative transfer was given by Madeline Hunter and Doug Russell:

- Positive transfer: Playing the piano aids in learning to play the organ.
- Negative transfer: Playing the piano slows learning to play the guitar because the hand movement is reversed.

Negative transfer lengthens the time required for a student to acquire the new knowledge. Three factors promote transfer. Teachers should use these three factors in developing their lesson plans to assist in positive transfer and avoid or minimize any negative transfer.

Teachers need to tie in to their students' prior learning and apply that prior learning to their current lessons so the current learning may be applied in the future. The three factors that promote transfer are:

- Similarity
- Degree of original learning
- Critical attributes

SIMILARITY

At some point in our lives, all of us have been to a McDonald's restaurant (some more frequently than others). All of us can recognize the famous golden arches from past learning experiences.

- If we see a colonial-style white clapboard building in Camden, Maine, that has a brass plaque containing the golden arches in raised relief; or
- if we see a Moorish-style structure in Granada, Spain, with golden arches in mosaic tiles on an outside wall,

through transfer, we would recognize both buildings as McDonald's restaurants based upon similarity. Similarity is the perception that "this is just like (or similar to)" something with which we are already familiar.

Teachers can promote positive transfer by highlighting the similarities:

- These problems are similar to the ones from last week.
- This group of poets is similar to the previous group, in that . . .
- This lab assignment is similar to last week's because . . .
- Tennis is similar to badminton because both . . .
- World War II is similar to World War I in that . . .

To avoid negative transfer, teachers need to highlight differences:

- The difference between the Impressionist painters and the Flemish artists is . . .
- Anticlines differ from synclines by . . .
- While the last group of poets focused on ____, the poets in this group . . .
- The difference between a digital clock and the older analog clocks is . . .

Teachers can also provide similarity for their students by creating and incorporating simulations into their lessons. Some commercial simulations are available through catalogs and can provide some very effective learning. Teachers can also create their own simulations through role-playing situations such as interviews, mock trials, re-creating original experiments, and decision-making and problem-solving situations. Instead of such activities as answering the questions at the back of a chapter, use activities such as:

- Creating a real-life skit for a French class using the new vocabulary.
- Role-playing the key moments in the Oval Office during the 1962 Cuban missile crisis.
- Applying mathematical formulas to designing additions to their homes.

Ideally, you want to progress to a point where the students themselves can draw similarities between the lesson and their own life experiences:

- Is there anything in this story that is a reflection on our lives today?
- How could you apply this geometry theorem at home?

To avoid confusion and negative transfer, effective teachers assist students in differentiating between similar words (Instructional Theory into Practice 1986):

Where:	About location, and contains the answer ("here")
Wear:	You decide what clothes to wear to school
Dessert:	Contains two "s's," as in strawberry shortcake
Desert:	Contains one "s," as in sand
Their:	Shows ownership and contains the word "heir" (someone who will own)
They're:	"They are" becomes "They're" when you replace the "a" with an apostrophe
There:	Location: There is the school

A young social studies teacher corrected "their/there" errors on student papers by drawing stick figures and labeling them "their." The teacher then drew an X and a wide arrow pointing to the X. She then labeled the arrow "there." The result was the visual: "their" equals people; "there" equals a place.

For the students to be able to differentiate between the similar words, each word is taught separately to a point that the students are successful. To avoid confusion, it is critical that the students have mastered the first word before the teacher moves on and introduces the second one. The next similar word is then introduced. If students become confused, the words are brought together and the differences are once again brought out by the teacher.

Similarity is also used by effective teachers for classroom management. For example, the day before a field trip to the John F.

Kennedy Library and Museum, a middle school teacher told the students:

- In school, you are quiet in the hallway when classes are in session.
- In school you do not run in the hallway.
- It is the same tomorrow at the John F. Kennedy Library and Museum.

The students recognize that the behavior is the same on the field trip as it is at school. The appropriate behavior transfers.

DEGREE OF ORIGINAL LEARNING

Anything worth teaching is worth teaching well. The more thoroughly something is learned, the greater the likelihood that the knowledge will transfer. Do not rush through or simply cover the material. *Teach to the objective(s). Teach for retention. Teach for transfer.* The degree of original learning is strongest if the elements presented in chapters 3, 4, and 5 are present in the lesson. Examples that provide meaning and are relevant to the students' daily lives are essential, as is constant assessment through planned questions. Go back to chapter 4 and again read the SPIRAL lesson; note how the examples clearly relate to the students' daily lives and provide meaning. These examples resulted in a high degree of original learning, retention, and transfer.

CRITICAL ATTRIBUTES

Critical attributes are the specific qualities that define something and differentiate it from everything else. For example:

- Eight equal sides and equal angles
- Red in color

It probably did not take very long, even without a visual representation, to identify the object as a stop sign. Its critical attributes are its:

- Shape
- Color

What about a sonnet? What are the critical attributes of a sonnet? What are the critical attributes of alliteration? What are the critical attributes of a monarchy? What are the critical attributes of a polynomial?

When students can identify the critical attributes of a thing, idea, or situation, they can transfer the learning to a new situation or new learning. Simply stated, the teacher needs to assist by:

- Identifying critical attributes
- Labeling critical attributes
- Teaching critical attributes

By teaching critical attributes, the teacher:

- Gives meaning to the learning
- Provides focus for students in the most important aspect of the learning
- Promotes both retention and transfer

Again, as in providing for retention, the selection of examples is critical. The same rules cited in the previous chapter apply; the examples must:

- Be clear
- Be relevant to the students' own lives

- Be planned in advance
- Be free from ambiguity or distractions (controversy or emotion)

Examples cannot be limited to one or two. Several examples should be cited. If you are teaching the concept of "metaphor," for example:

- List several examples starting with the simple and obvious.
- Cite more complex examples.
- Have the students apply the critical attributes and find additional examples.
- Have the students generate their own examples.

The last point is proof of the students' ability to transfer what they have learned. In the example cited, the teacher would later differentiate between metaphor, simile, and personification, after all of those terms had been taught and the students had demonstrated success. See the opposite page for a worksheet that will assist you in teaching for transfer.

TRANSFER WORKSHEET

Activity: _____

Identify a specific idea or concept that you want to transfer.

Identify any similarities with previous learning.

Identify any similarities with student life.

Identify any appropriate simulations.

Identify the critical attributes of the idea or concept.

Identify several appropriate examples from simple to complex.

6

EVALUATION

L ook at your objective(s). Just like everything you did in teaching, the lesson was related to the objective(s); everything you do to evaluate your students' learning must also relate directly to your objectives(s). Your objective may be:

- The learner will describe the various complex causes of World War II.
- The learner will explain the American strategy for winning the war in the Pacific.
- The learner will describe the various types of lava flows.
- The learner will explain the critical attributes of a sonnet.
- The learner will identify four different polygons.

In these cases, everything you do in evaluation should focus on measuring the extent to which you students can:

- Describe the various complex causes of World War II.
- Explain the American strategy for winning the war in the Pacific.

- Describe the various types of lava flows.
- Explain the critical attributes of a sonnet.
- Describe and differentiate between the various polygons.

Your evaluation should not be limited to a test and needs to include homework and quizzes. There should be a direct relationship between the objective(s) and the homework, and between the homework and the quizzes. Likewise, there is a direct relationship between the quizzes and the test.

The purpose of the homework is *not* to keep them (and you) busy but to prepare the students for the quizzes. The purpose of the quizzes is to show both the teacher and the students whether they have achieved the objective(s) and are prepared for the test. The homework is a preview and preparation for the quizzes; likewise, the quizzes are a preview and preparation for the test. To further illustrate this concept, see figure 6.1.

How much emphasis was placed on the art of test construction in your undergraduate teacher-preparation courses? How many courses did you take that emphasized how to design good tests? Do you feel adequately prepared to design a good test? It is one area in which teachers often do not feel adequately trained, yet it is an essential part of teaching! Some general comments on tests:

- Generally, the more items or questions a test has, the more reliable the test.
- Consider giving a practice test early in the course. Your students have no idea what to expect until they take your first test.
- More frequent testing over a smaller amount of material will provide better results than fewer tests over more material.

OBJECTIVE(S)

HOMEWORK

QUIZZES

TEST

Figure 6.1.   How It Fits Together

- Consider what adjustments will be required for students with disabilities or whose primary language is not English.
- Well-written tests adequately measure the students' understanding of the content that was taught.
- Well-written tests focus on the objectives. The objectives that were taught should form the basic outline of your test.
- Avoid writing the test all at once. Each day, write some items that match the objectives that were taught.
- Place several questions at the beginning of the test that you expect all students to be able to answer correctly. This will build confidence.

- Give students suggestions on how to study. Studies show that students prepare according to how they expect to be tested. They will memorize details if they anticipate being tested on facts; they will focus on understanding and applying information if they expect a test requiring problem solving (Davis n.d.).

TYPES OF TEST QUESTIONS

What type of test questions are you going to develop? Generally your tests should consist of not more than three sections, each section focusing on a different type of question (for example, a section of multiple-choice questions, a section of short-answer questions, and an essay question). Each type of question has both advantages and limitations.

Multiple-choice Questions

Multiple-choice questions:

- Can be used for higher level thinking skills as well as factual recall
- Require minimal student writing
- Can be corrected quickly
- Require ample time to properly construct

In constructing multiple-choice questions:

- The initial part (statement), known as the "stem," should be written as a question rather than as an incomplete statement.
  Example: How are alloys ordinarily produced?

Instead of: Alloys are ordinarily produced by . . . (Clay 2001, 15)

- Rather than include the same words in each choice, include those words in the stem (Clay 2001, 15).
  Example: The hunter-gatherers' way of life made it impossible for them to live in:
    A. groups
    B. cold climates
    C. permanent dwellings
    D. forests
  Instead of: The hunter-gatherers' way of life made it impossible:
    A. for them to live in groups
    B. for them to live in cold climates
    C. for them to live in permanent dwellings
    D. for them to live in forests

- Avoid giving the answer by tipping the students with "a" or "an" in the stem (Clay 2001, 17).
  Example: All of the following were characteristics of Athenian democracy *except*:
    A. an executive branch
    B. political power limited to its citizens
    C. leaders chosen by the aristocracy
    D. laws proposed by and voted upon by citizens
  Instead of: All of the following were characteristics of Athenian democracy *except an*:
    A. executive branch
    B. political power limited to its citizens
    C. leaders chosen by the aristocracy
    D. laws proposed by and voted upon by citizens

- Avoid testing for trivia.
  Example: While aboard ship in the 1830s, Charles Darwin made observations on:
    A. societal groupings
    B. economic phenomena

C. plant and animal life

D. the heavens

Instead of: Charles Darwin made observations of plant and animal life of _____ while aboard the _____ in the 1830s.

A. North America, USS Liberty

B. South America, USS Liberty

C. North America, HMS Beagle

D. South America, HMS Beagle

- Present a definite, explicit, and singular question in the stem (Clay 2001, 15).

Example: The study of living organisms is:

Instead of: Biology is the study of:

- Include multiple-choice questions that measure higher order thinking skills involving concepts or generalizations.

Example: An appropriate conclusion from studying the American Civil War, World War I, and World War II is that:

A. Civilian populations are not direct targets.

B. Weapons change, but strategy does not change.

C. Strategically the military prepares to fight the last war again.

D. Defensive strategy generally prevails over offensive.

Instead of a simple recall question such as: Which of the following statements about World War II is *not* accurate:

A. The aircraft carrier replaced the battleship as the dominant naval weapon.

B. Strategically, military powers other than Germany were prepared to fight the previous war again.

C. Civilian populations were not specifically targeted.

D. The turning point of the war in both the European and Asian stages occurred practically simultaneously.

- When using negative statements in the stem, italicize, underline, and/or capitalize the negative word (Clay 2001, 16). Example: Which of the following is *not* a characteristic of a sonnet?
  Instead of: Which of the following is not a characteristic of a sonnet?

Other tips on writing multiple-choice questions:

- Use terms in the stem, not among the possible answers, when testing on definitions.
- Keep all of the possible answers in the same format (all one word or one phrase or one sentence).
- Make all of the possible answers relatively the same length (the correct one is frequently longer).
- Randomly distribute the correct answer. When you finish the multiple-choice section, A, B, C, and D responses should be evenly distributed (Clay 2001, 15–16).

Matching Items

Matching items:

- Are useful for knowledge level questions
- Are useful for matching:
  Causes with effects
  Terms with definitions
  Problems with solutions
  Phrases with phrases
  Parts with the whole

- Require minimal test space and preparation time
- Are useful for material with high factual content
- Are difficult to use for higher level thinking

Tips on writing matching items:

- Keep the lists brief (no more than ten to fifteen items in each column).
- Limit the response column to a single word or short phrase.
- Keep the possible correct responses to one per item.
- Keep the section on one page (do not let it run over to the next page).
- Keep all of the responses in a related category (do not mix "apples and oranges"). If the item is matching works to their author, all of the responses should be authors (not years or types of works) (Clay 2001, 15–16).

Fill-in-the-Blank Items

Fill-in-the-blank items:

- Are useful for recall and memorization of factual information
- Are good for who, what, when, and where content
- Require students to know rather than recognize the correct response
- May have more than one answer
- Take time to correct
- Are difficult to use for higher level thinking

Tips on writing fill-in-the-blank items:

- Omit significant words only when writing the statement. Example: Every atom has a central core called a(n) _____.

Instead of: Every atom has a central _____ called a nucleus (Clay 2001, 36).

- Do not have so many blanks in the statement that the meaning is lost.
  Example: The Emperors were to Rome as the _____ were to Egypt and as the _____ were to the Hittites.
  Instead of: The _____ were to Rome as the _____ were to Egypt and as the _____ were to the Hittites.

Essay Test Items

Essay test items:

- Are applicable for the higher level thinking skills of application, analysis, synthesis, and evaluation
- Require more study time for the students
- Are relatively easy for the teacher to write
- Are time-consuming to score
- Scoring is subjective and possibly unreliable
- Can limit the amount of material tested

Research shows that students study more efficiently for an essay type of exam than for objective test items. The students are required to focus on broad issues, concepts, and interrelationships rather than factual data. Unfortunately, essay tests generally favor students with the best handwriting and allow students the opportunity to ramble in hopes of hitting the desired response (Clay 2001, 38).

Tips on writing essay questions:

- Refer to your Bloom's taxonomy list of verbs for one appropriate for your question.

- Be specific in what task you are requesting. Simply asking the student to "discuss" is too vague.

Example: Compare Tobias Smollett's view of daily life in England in *The Expedition of Humphry Clinker* with that of Charles Dickens in *The Old Curiosity Shop.*
Instead of: Discuss the writings of Charles Dickens.

- Use a specific, standard scoring device. Hopefully your school has established rubrics throughout all grades and subject areas.

- Assist your students in preparing for an essay question. Before the first test with an essay question,
  Have the students practice writing responses to essay questions. Discuss how to structure the essay.
  Show examples of high-scoring essay responses and low-scoring responses (Clay 2001, 44).

How much time should you plan for your test? Generally, you can use the following as a guide:

- Thirty seconds per true-false item
- One minute per multiple-choice item
- Two minutes per short-answer item
- Ten to fifteen minutes per essay question
- Five to ten minutes for the students to check their answers
- Three to four times as long as it takes you to take the test (Clay 2001, 52).

Now, before you begin to type your test:

- Ask what you are testing—skills, concepts, and generalizations, or trivia?
- Review your objective(s), the homework that was assigned, and the quizzes that were given.

Assuming you answered your own question by stating that you were testing skills, concepts, and generalizations rather than trivia, begin to develop your test. If you are testing concepts and generalizations, you can ask some meaningful factual (not trivial) questions. Two-thirds of your test should focus on concepts and generalizations. Your objective may be:

- Explain the American strategy for winning the war in the Pacific.

In this case, some conceptual questions might focus on:

- Island hopping
- Amphibious assault
- Airpower

Some generalization questions might focus on:

- The crucial point in an amphibious assault was the securing of a beachhead.
- The closer American forces got to Japan, the higher the casualties for both sides.
- The aircraft carrier replaced the battleship as the major weapon on the seas.

Some relevant factual questions might include:

- Sequencing of events, such as Pearl Harbor, the Battle of Midway, the assault on Guadalcanal, the assault on Iwo Jima, and the bombing of Hiroshima
- The relationship between the emperor, the Zaibatsu, and the military
- Key personalities such as Emperor Hirohito, General Tojo, and Admiral Nimitz

An example of trivial questions would be:

- Any single specific date(s) (except landmark dates such as December 7, 1941)
- The number of losses in any battle(s)

As you write each test item, ask yourself if it relates directly back to your quizzes, homework, and the objective(s). Also ask yourself:

- Is the question clear and concise?
- Is the question written in the language of the learning?
- Is the question valid?

In the words of Charlie Brown, from Charles Schulz's comic strip "Peanuts," "Taking a true-false test is like having the wind at your back." If you are thinking of including any true-false questions or developing a totally true-false test, stop. Ask yourself, why? How valid are true-false tests? Do they accurately measure learning? You can strengthen true-false questions by allowing more space between the questions, and at the end of each true-false statement add the word: "explain." In addition to selecting either "true" or "false," the student is now required to explain his or her answer.

The master teacher constructs multipart tests, with each part measuring the same material in different ways:

- Multiple-choice questions
- Short-answer questions
- Fill-in-the-blank questions
- Sequencing
- Essay

Multiple-choice questions should be designed so that students who have an understanding of the material select the correct answer; those students unfamiliar with the material should be likely to select an incorrect answer. Avoid making the correct response too obviously the only one that is appropriate. Some, although not *all*, of the questions should test knowledge and comprehension. You also need to include questions that require students to use higher level thinking skills (for example, analyze a relationship).

You should develop your own tests rather than use the premade tests that come with the textbook. Your tests reflect how and what you taught. You taught the class; the book did not teach the students. Since you will not teach the course exactly the same any two consecutive years, your test will need to be changed according to what and how you taught each time you teach the course.

When you have finished developing your test, print a single copy. Again, review each question and ask:

- Does the question relate to the objective?
- Is the question clear and concise?
- Is the question written in the same language as the learning?
- Is the question valid?

When administering the test, first instruct the students to place their pens and/or pencils flat on the desk. Have the students read through the test prior to answering any of the test questions. Monitor the test. Do not sit and read. Do not grade the last-period class's test. You should only monitor the test. Period. After the tests have been collected and graded, there is one more important task remaining:

- Do a test analysis.

Record the number of students who gave an incorrect response for each question. For any question that was missed by a significant number of students, ask yourself:

- Is the question vague, misleading, or confusing?

If there is nothing wrong with the test question, then you must ask yourself:

- Was something wrong with the teaching?
- Why did several students respond incorrectly?

A totally unacceptable response to the last question is "I put it out there. If they did not get it, it is their fault." *No, the responsibility is yours.*

One more question concerning questions missed by a significant number of students:

- Is the learning necessary for future learning?

If the learning is necessary for future learning, then you need to reteach that portion of the material.

Also consider the frequency of testing. Remember those undergraduate or graduate courses where the professor only gave one test—the final exam. Did you prefer a professor who gave one, two, three, or several exams over the length of the course? There is an obvious relationship between the amount of material covered by the test and the results of the test. More frequent testing shortens the period between tests, resulting in a higher rate of retention and higher test scores.

When you have finished scoring the test:

- Return them the next time the class meets.
- Do not put the scores on the front or back of the test where they will show. Write the score on an inside page.

Test scores are private and confidential. The students may share them if they choose (and they will). You must maintain confidentiality. In the same manner, if you wish to post test scores, do not use names or initials. Assign each student a random number (not consecutive numbers alphabetically).

Over the past fifteen years, portfolios have emerged as a means of assessing student performance and progress. With the increase in classroom computers and computer labs in elementary, middle, and high schools, electronic portfolios have taken preference over paper portfolios. Electronic portfolios do not require the many boxes, file cabinets, or closets for storage that paper portfolios do. Electronic portfolios may also be enhanced with voice, music, digital pictures, and graphics.

Electronic portfolios are used in schools from the primary through the secondary levels for assessment and for display. An assessment portfolio is a collection of the student's work that is reflective of his or her progress and performance for various learning standards. Display portfolios are designed for the purpose of showcasing the students' work at events such as an open house or parent conferences. Display portfolios, however, contain only the best of the students' work.

Vermont is one of the leaders in portfolio development. A study conducted in public schools there indicated that the teachers using portfolios reported:

- An increase in the level of problem-solving and higher level learning.
- A change in the way the teachers thought about their teaching (Dowling 2000, 4).

Portfolios may contain:

- Journal entries and reflective writing
- Peer reviews
- Artwork
- Diagrams, charts, graphs
- Group work/reports
- Rough drafts to finished essays
- Videos
- Music
- Digital photographs

Portfolios are an excellent means to document progress and learning over time. Electronic portfolios have countless advantages over paper portfolios in both the required storage and the variety of items that may be included. Most importantly, they have proven to be useful to increase students' abilities in problem solving and higher level thinking.

7

EFFECTIVE TEACHING RESEARCH

A considerable amount of research on effective teaching has been conducted over the past thirty years. The compilation of this research provides a definite description of the "best practices" in teaching and learning.

Successful teachers demonstrate a thorough knowledge of the best practices in teaching and learning, hence their success in advancing the learning of their students. Any trained observer with a knowledge of the effective teaching research can sit in a successful teacher's class and point to the relationship between the actions of the teacher and the compiled research. All teachers and all supervisors of teachers need to possess a thorough understanding of the research on effective teaching.

In chapter 3, research from scholars such as Kindsvatter, Wilen, and Ishler (1988); Sindelar, Bursuck, and Halle (1986); and others was reviewed. The research in that chapter pertained to questioning as it related to teaching to the objective. This chapter reviews research that relates to the broader aspects of teaching and learning.

Chapter 1 focused on classroom management, as good classroom management must exist in order for teaching and learning to occur. Research by Riner (as cited in Jones-Hamilton 2001) indicated that the critical variables of effective teaching included the management of student behavior and the management of instructional time as well as the presentation and facilitation of instruction, and noninstructional duties (Jones-Hamilton 2001, 1). In addition, Olivia and Pawless found that effective teachers consistently monitored student behavior and dealt with inappropriate behaviors immediately (as cited in Jones-Hamilton 2001, 1). Ellet reported that effective management of instructional time *and* student behavior were necessary elements of effective teaching (as cited in Jones-Hamilton 2001, 2). Research, common sense, and experience support the idea that classroom management is an essential part of teaching and that effective teachers consistently handle inappropriate behavior.

Chapter 2 identified four essential components:

- An initial sponge activity
- A statement of the lesson's objective(s)
- Frequent checks to ensure student understanding
- Closure at the end of the period

Madeline Hunter and Doug Russell (1987) used the term "anticipatory set" for beginning a class by focusing the students' attention on the lesson. Their research concluded that this practice was common in the lessons of effective teachers.

Dr. Leslie Jones-Hamilton of the University of North Carolina, Wilmington, Center for Teaching Excellence determined that planning is essential in classroom teaching, and that the planning included written goals and stated objectives (Jones-Hamilton 2001, 2).

Rosenshine included a short statement of goals (objectives) as one characteristic of effective teaching in his extensive research (as cited in Ellis and Worthington 1994, 82). More of his extensive research on effective teaching practices will be presented later. In a comprehensive report summarizing the research on effective teaching practices, Kathleen Cotton (1995) reported that effective teachers:

- Implement lessons focusing on specifics (objectives) that students are expected to learn.
- Facilitate learning by communicating instructional objectives to students with the specifics regarding what is to be learned.
- Communicate goals (objectives), rationales, lesson structures, and directions, thereby increasing student achievement.

Research does support the fact that sharing the objectives with students has a positive impact upon achievement! Inform the students what they are supposed to know or be able to do! As stated previously in chapter 3, do not keep your desired outcomes a secret; do not make the students guess what they are supposed to know or be able to do. If you want success, share your objective(s).

Rosenshine concluded that the effective teaching research showed a consistent pattern of instruction for teaching skills and concepts. Effective teachers define the skills and explain the concepts to be learned, and present information in small steps.

Rosenshine (cited in Ellis and Worthington 1994, 78) reported that when teaching skills and concepts, effective teachers:

- Begin each lesson with a concise statement of goals (objectives)
- Begin each lesson with a short review of relevant previous materials
- Present new information in small steps with practice after each step

- Provide clear and detailed instructions
- Provide active practice for all students
- Ask many questions to check for understanding and obtain responses from all students
- Guide students through initial practice
- Provide systematic feedback
- Monitor student seatwork

In his research, Rosenshine found that the teaching was more effective when students received immediate feedback. Immediate corrections assisted students in reaching mastery levels.

Rosenshine also reported that when monitoring student seatwork, teacher interactions with the students should be brief (thirty seconds at most). Long explanations indicate that the initial teaching was not effective. If this occurs with several students, it would be best to stop the seatwork and reteach the material.

In her extensive compilation of effective teaching research, Kathleen Cotton reports on several noted and relevant findings in addition to those mentioned previously. Some of these are listed here. Effective teachers (Cotton 1995, 9–15):

- Use whole-group instruction when introducing new skills or concepts.
- Use small-group instruction to strengthen learning, with students placed according to achievement level.
- Use heterogeneous cooperative learning groups in a manner that provides both group rewards and individual accountability.
- Pace the lesson so that is neither too easy nor too difficult for most students, while providing adaptations for the faster and slower learners.
- Give elementary students short homework assignments to build study habits and longer assignments of forty-five min-

utes to two hours to high school students in order to reinforce learning.

- Show the relationship between the current learning and previous lessons, pointing out the key concepts or skills that were taught earlier.
- Have an expectation that all students are to contribute to the classroom discussions and activities.
- Correct and return homework promptly to provide feedback.
- Reteach essential lesson content until the students demonstrate that they have learned it.
- Teach study skills.
- Teach strategies for problem solving, decision making, and hypothesizing.
- Plan their questions to focus on key elements in the lesson.
- Ask a combination of lower and higher order questions to stimulate thinking and to check for understanding.
- Serve as facilitators and coaches rather than lecturers.
- Hold students accountable for assignments and class participation.

We also know that teachers who use a variety of methods were more effective than teachers who only extended one method of instruction, and that engaging students in learning (active learning) by giving them the opportunity to practice the skill or concept resulted in greater retention.

Lecturing is a valuable part of teaching but should not be used exclusively or for lengthy periods of time. The longer a teacher lectures in a class period, the less effective it becomes as a means of teaching. Limit lectures to thirty minutes or less, and provide time for the students to become actively engaged in practicing the skill/concept. Even the most accomplished and entertaining lectures cannot effectively hold the attention of students of any grade level for a length of time much past thirty minutes. Highly skilled and gifted lecturers who were confronted with periods of eighty to ninety minutes with the introduction of a "block schedule" discovered that they could not simply teach two lessons (give two lectures) in the longer block. No matter how entertaining a teacher might be, he or she cannot lecture effectively for eighty to ninety minutes.

The adoption of block schedules by schools forced teachers to adopt a different way of teaching. The French and math teachers cited in chapter 3 are two examples of teachers who changed their teaching methods and strategies by incorporating activities that involved active learning. Another example is a history teacher who replaced lectures with activities such as:

- Writing journals for the period studied
- Writing a newspaper article or a television newscast about the event
- Conducting a mock trial
- Writing and presenting a dramatization

REVIEW: RESEARCH INDICATES EFFECTIVE TEACHERS

- Monitor student behavior
- Adjust inappropriate behavior immediately
- Begin class with a sponge activity
- Provide a statement of their objective(s)
- Teach new information in small steps
- Provide clear and detailed instructions
- Provide practice
- Guide students through the initial practice
- Check for understanding with all students
- Provide immediate feedback
- Monitor the students' seatwork
- Use a variety of methods in each lesson
- Maximize time on task

8

PUTTING
IT TOGETHER

As you have already discovered, contrary to a fairly common perception, teaching is not easy. A considerable amount of work is involved in preparing a single lesson. Students are not the eager, enthusiastic receptacles craving knowledge that novices anticipate. You will find some students to be apathetic! Most of the individuals entering teaching from business or industry leave teaching within the first three years. Many underestimated the amount of work involved in teaching; others did not enter teaching because they cared for kids, but because it was simply a job and, as everyone knows, anyone can teach.

Here are some tips before you venture into the classroom:

- First, reread chapter 1 on classroom management. If you do not like children or young adults, find another career!
- If you cannot consistently manage a classroom by following the procedures outlined in chapter 1, find another career!
- If you cannot walk into the classroom and take charge, find another career!
- If you are intimidated by a classroom full of students, find another career!

- If, in the classroom, your speech and body language convey timidity rather than confidence and control, find another career! Although it sounds like a terrible analogy, students are like dogs in that both can sense fear.
- Your success in the classroom as a college student is irrelevant. Your college grade point average is irrelevant. If you cannot manage a classroom, and manage that classroom in an appropriate manner, you *cannot teach*!

Teaching is both a science and an art. The science of teaching can be learned from supervisors, mentors, and research on effective teaching. The structuring of effective lessons is the science of teaching. The science of teaching can be taught and new teachers can learn to be effective presenters of lessons. The art of teaching is innate; it includes a person's ability to relate to their students, to consistently manage a classroom while providing an atmosphere that promotes learning, and to convey and transmit their enthusiasm for the subject to their students. Effective teachers have a specific persona that enables them to be effective in their relationships with their students.

Procedures for effectively managing a classroom can be outlined, as they are in chapter 1. The persona that effective teachers possess cannot be outlined or taught. The art of teaching cannot be taught; it either exists within or it does not exist. *Effective teachers can relate to and like, respect, and care about their students.* They may have been in the classroom for three years or thirty-three years, but this quality exists, and will never change; it is this quality that endears them to their students. This quality is the reason why these teachers are respected by their students and the reason why these teachers are effective in classroom management. These teachers have always followed the procedures outlined in chapter 1, instinctively.

PLANNING YOUR LESSONS AND TESTS

In terms of the science of teaching, let's consider your planning for the next lesson that you will be teaching.

- What do you want your students to be able to demonstrate as a result of the lesson?
- What is the skill or concept that you want learned?

Based on the above, write your objective(s).

- Ask yourself, "What is the best way to teach this?"
  Based upon this, plan the activities that you will use to teach the objective(s). Incorporate active learning activities, minimizing the amount of lecture time.
- What is your sponge activity?
  Identify what activity the students will engage in upon entering the classroom to focus their attention on the lesson.
- How are you going to check the students' level of understanding?
  Plan the specific questions that you will ask to determine whether the students understand. Identify the points in the lesson at which you will check the level of understanding (every three to eight minutes).
- What examples will you use to teach the skill or concept?
  Plan the specific examples that you will use in teaching the skill or concept. Examples that are clear and concise and that relate to the students' daily lives increase both retention and transfer.
- Can you design a mnemonic device?
  Can you create an acronym or sentence to assist in retention?
- Identify the critical attributes of the skill or concept that you want learned. Label the critical attributes that you will identify for the students.

- How will you provide closure?
  Plan activities for closure. Do not let the last three to five minutes go unused! Once again, use the time to measure the level of understanding. You need to be certain that all students have met the objective.
- What homework will you assign?
  Plan the homework assignments. Do the assignments match the objective(s)? Do the assignments lead to the quizzes and tests?
- Develop your quizzes.
  Be certain that your quizzes are based upon the objective(s) and the homework. Do your quizzes provide a preview of the test? Do they show you and the students the extent to which they are prepared for the test?
- Develop your test.
  Make certain that you are testing skills and concepts and not trivia. Make certain that each question relates to the objectives. Make certain that you develop a multipart test. The objectives are then measured through several questions of different types.
- Plan on an analysis of the test results.
  Look at the number of students who incorrectly responded to each test item. When a significant number miss the same test item, you have to ask yourself why.
- Plan for the next time.
  At the end of each day, ask yourself "How can I teach this lesson better?" What worked well? What did not go well? Why? Take ten minutes of "quiet time" at the end of each day before leaving the building. Use the time to reflect on the day's classes, and make notes on what you need to change to improve the lesson(s).

The most effective and successful teachers are their own best critics. They constantly ask these questions, no matter how long they have been teaching. These teachers are always striving to improve their teaching, day by day, lesson by lesson, and year by year. Successful teachers are constantly revising their courses' lessons, and do not teach them exactly the same any two consecutive years. As a result, their tests are also changing to some degree from year to year.

CURRICULUM/LESSON DESIGN AND TIMING

You will be shocked at the amount of time you spend in your first year preparing your lessons. The first-year teacher has to:

- Become familiar with the curriculum and state standards
- Design appropriate lessons, assignments, and tests
- Learn how much can be taught successfully in a given length of class time

All of these take time and are part of an ongoing learning process throughout the school year. You will find that some lessons will go better in some of your classes than in others. You will find that in some classes you can complete the lesson as planned in one period, while you are unable to complete the entire lesson in another class. Each class is different. Make sure you use class time appropriately, allow time for closure, and teach from bell to bell.

USE YOUR COLLEAGUES, IMMEDIATE SUPERVISOR, AND BUILDING PRINCIPAL

Solicit ideas from your colleagues. What are they doing in their classrooms that is successful? How do they manage students with whom you have difficulty? Do these students respond differently to these teachers? What suggestions do they have for your lesson? When they taught the same lesson, what did they do to promote learning, retention, and transfer?

Observe the successful teachers in your building. Do not confine yourself to only your department. Excellent teaching is excellent teaching, whether it is in a Spanish, English, or science class. Why are these teachers so successful? Observe how they treat their students. Observe how they manage their classrooms. What comparisons do you see between their teaching and the effective teaching research?

Ask a colleague to videotape one of your classes; the tape is to be for *your use only*. Take the tape home and watch it several times. Critique your own teaching. You will likely be surprised at what you see. More than likely, you will ask, "Did I really do/say that?" Compare your actions to that of the teachers whom you observed. What was missing from your class? What should not have been done in your class? You should be your toughest critic. The most successful teachers have always been the most critical of their own performance.

Today, most schools have created mentor programs, with experienced teachers serving as mentors for new teachers. Mentors serve as valuable assets, as they can help guide new teachers from preparing for the first day to dealing with parent issues and grading. It is preferred that mentors and teachers work in the same grade level and/or subject area. Where mentor systems do not yet exist, it is highly recommended that they be established by the building principal working collaboratively with his or her faculty. Volunteers should be sought out and also solicited, with the principal recruiting from the most successful teachers in the building.

Obviously any successful mentoring program needs some common standards. All mentors need to be familiar with, and teach in accordance with, the effective teaching research that has been compiled since the 1980s. The summation of this research establishes the standard for what are considered to be the school's or district's best practices.

Invite your colleagues to observe you and ask for their suggestions to improve the lesson. Also ask your immediate supervisor and principal to observe your teaching, and solicit their suggestions. Do not be afraid to be creative and try something new and different. Not everything you do will be successful, but do not let that stop you from being creative. Do not expect your students to be wildly excited about every lesson! Some lessons will go better than others. Learn from the experience, and keep trying!

Finally, always remember: Good teaching does not just happen —it is the result of good planning!

REFERENCES

Active Learning Team. N.d. "What Is Active Learning?" Abilene Christian University's Adams Center for Teaching Excellence. www.acu.edu/cte/activelearning/whyusel.htm (accessed January 5, 2006).

Becker, Henry J., Jason L. Ravitz, and Yan Tien Wong. 1999. "Teacher and Teacher-Directed Student Use of Computers and Software." Center for Research on Information Technology and Organizations, University of California, Irvine, and University of Minnesota. www.crito.uci.edu/tlc/findings/computeruse.

Bloom, Benjamin, ed. 1956. *Taxonomy of Educational Objectives: Cognitive Domain.* New York: David McKay.

Brophy, J. E., and C. M. Evertson. 1976. *Learning from Teaching: A Developmental Perspective.* Boston: Allyn & Bacon.

Clay, Ben. 2001. "Is This a Trick Question? A Short Guide to Writing Effective Test Questions." Kansas Curriculum Center, Kansas Department of Education, www.kcterc.ksde.org (accessed January 25, 2006).

Collins, John, ed. 2005, July. "School Improvement through Writing across the Curriculum." Paper presented at the Harvard Graduate School of Education's Principals' Institute.

Cotton, Kathleen. 1995. *Effective Schooling Practices: A Research Synthesis −1995 Update.* Portland, Ore.: Northwest Regional Educational Laboratory.

Davis, Barbara Gross. "Quizzes, Tests and Exams." University of California, Berkeley. www.teaching.berkeley.edu (accessed January 25, 2006).

Dowling, Laura J. 2000, May 12. "Using Electronic Portfolios: A Description and Analysis for Implementation in SIGNET Classes at Woodbridge Middle School, Virginia." www.dowlingcentral.com/gradschool/Edu6150/FinalPaper-EDUC6150-LauraJDowling.htm (accessed January 14, 2006), 4.

Drummond, Tom. 2003. *A Brief Summary of the Best Practices in Teaching.* Seattle: North Seattle Community College.

Ellis, E. S., and K. Lenz. 1992. *Critical Features of Effective Strategy Instruction.* Denver: Love.

Ellis, E. S., and L. A. Worthington. 1994. "Research Synthesis on Effective Teaching Principles and the Design of Quality Tools for Educators." University of Oregon, Eugene.

Hunter, Madeline. 1987. Paper presented at the Instructional Theory into Practice Program, University of Wisconsin, Green Bay.

Jones-Hamilton, Leslie. 2001. *Measuring Effective Teaching.* Wilmington: University of North Carolina Center for Teaching Excellence.

Kindsvatter, Richard, William Wilen, and Margaret Ishler. 1988. *The Dynamics of Effective Teaching.* New York: Longman.

Reeves, Douglas. 2005, July. "Leadership for Learning: Transforming Theory into Action for Improved Achievement and Educational Equity." Paper presented at the Harvard Graduate School of Education's Principals' Institute.

Rogers, Spence. 2005, October. "Assessment Strategies That Teach and Increase Achievement." Paper presented at the ASCD Conference on Teaching and Learning.

Russell, Douglas. 1987. Paper presented at the Instructional Theory into Practice Program, University of Wisconsin, Green Bay.

Stevenson, Dana, Martha Berner, and Carol Brust. 2001, January. "Bloom's Taxonomy User's Guide Adapted from the Williamsburg Model." Cajon Valley Union School District and PAR Consultants.

Wiggins, Grant. 2005, October. "Less Teaching, More Assessing: Learning via Feedback." Paper presented at the ASCD Conference on Teaching and Learning.

Youth Learn Institute. 2003. "The Art of Asking Good Questions." Morino Institute. www.youthlearn.org/teaching/questions.asp (accessed January 5, 2006).

ABOUT THE AUTHOR

James L. Conro began his career in education as a social studies teacher at Grant High School in Fox Lake, Illinois (1969–1974). He completed his master's degree in education administration at Northern Illinois University in 1974.

His additional studies in education administration were at Winona State University, the University of Wisconsin–Eau Claire, the University of Wisconsin–Green Bay, the University of Vermont, and Harvard University's Principals' Institute.

He has served as a building principal in Wisconsin and in New England since 1974. His philosophy of effective teaching stems from his educational experiences in the U.S. Army, his training in "instructional theory into practice" at the University of Wisconsin–Eau Claire, classes with Madeline Hunter and Doug Russell at the University of Wisconsin–Green Bay, and more than thirty years of experience with classroom teachers.